Comparing G-20 Reform of the Over-the-Counter Derivatives Markets

James K. Jackson
Specialist in International Trade and Finance

Rena S. Miller
Analyst in Financial Economics

February 19, 2013

Congressional Research Service

7-5700

www.crs.gov

R42961

Summary

Derivatives, or financial instruments whose value is based on an underlying asset, played a key role in the financial crisis of 2008-2009. Congress directly addressed the governance of the derivatives markets through the Dodd-Frank Wall Street Reform and Consumer Protection Act (Dodd-Frank; P.L. 111-203; July 21, 2010). This Act, in Title VII, sought to bring the largely unregulated over-the-counter (OTC) derivatives markets under greater regulatory control and scrutiny. Pillars of this approach included mandating that certain OTC derivatives be subject to central clearing, such as through a clearinghouse, which involves posting margin to cover potential losses; greater transparency through trading on exchanges or exchange-like facilities; and reporting trades to a repository, among other reforms.

In the debates over Dodd-Frank and in subsequent years, many in Congress have raised the following important questions: If the United States takes stronger regulatory action than other countries, will business in these OTC derivatives markets shift overseas? Since OTC derivatives markets are global in nature, could derivatives trading across borders, or business for U.S. financial firms that engage in these trades, be disrupted if other countries do not adopt similar regulatory frameworks? The first step in addressing these congressional concerns is to examine the degree to which other major countries have adopted similar legislation and regulation as the United States, particularly in light of commitments from the Group of Twenty nations (G-20) to adopt certain derivatives reforms.

Following the financial crisis, G-20 leaders (generally political heads of state) established a reform agenda and priorities within that agenda for regulating and overseeing OTC derivatives. The G-20 as an organization has no enforcement capabilities, but relies on the members themselves to implement reforms. According to recent surveys, most members are making progress in meeting the self-imposed goal of implementing major reforms in derivatives markets. Only the United States appears to have met all the reforms endorsed by the G-20 members within the desired timeframe of year-end 2012.

The European Union (EU), Japan, Hong Kong, and the United States have each taken significant steps towards implementing legislation requiring central clearing. However, in most of these jurisdictions legislation has not yet been followed up with technical implementing regulations for the requirements to become effective, according to the Financial Stability Board (FSB), which conducts the surveys. Most authorities surveyed estimated that a significant proportion of interest rate derivatives would be centrally cleared by year-end 2012, but they were less confident of progress for other asset classes. The EU appeared to be making progress in its G-20 derivatives regulatory commitments, particularly in central clearing and trade repository-reporting requirements, but at a slower pace than the United States, according to the FSB. This may be due in part to the need for legislation to be passed by individual national legislatures even when agreed broadly by the EU. As of October 2012, however, only the United States had adopted legislation requiring standardized derivatives to be traded on exchanges and electronic platforms.

This report examines the G-20 recommendations for reforming OTC derivatives markets and presents the result of self-assessment surveys measuring the performance of G-20 members and some FSB members to date in meeting their commitments. The Appendix to the report presents more detailed information on the status of individual jurisdictions in implementing the G-20-endorsed reforms. The Glossary defines key international bodies and related financial terms and concepts.

Contents

Figures

Tables

Appendixes

Contacts

Background

Financial derivatives are widely used throughout the economy by financial firms, corporations, farmers, and investors to serve a number of different purposes. A broad set of factors are responsible for the 2008-2009 financial crisis, but derivatives played a key role in the crisis by fueling a housing bubble and enabling large scale systemic risk in the financial system. Congress plays a major role in the derivatives market by passing laws and regulations that define the nature of derivatives market activity and through its oversight role over the major regulators of the derivatives markets.

The 2008-2009 financial crisis spurred policymakers from a range of countries, spearheaded by the G-20,[1] to commit their countries to reforming domestic and international rules governing the over-the-counter (OTC) derivatives markets.[2] Most assessments generally agree that a broad set of factors played a role in the financial crisis and in the ensuing sovereign debt crisis in Europe. However, actions by investors in the derivatives markets likely aggravated the financial crisis, required billions in government assistance to American International Group, Inc. (AIG) and other financial firms to cover losses associated with credit default swaps (CDS),[3] and played a key role in destabilizing financial markets. In addition, public and congressional attention has continued to focus on derivatives markets as a result of the key role derivatives played in worsening Greece's financial crisis and the roughly $6 billion in derivatives-trading losses in 2012 reported by JP Morgan.[4]

---

[1] For additional information about the G-20 see: CRS Report R40977, *The G-20 and International Economic Cooperation: Background and Implications for Congress*, by Rebecca M. Nelson.

[2] Derivatives contracts are characterized by the way they are traded. Over-the-counter derivatives are contracts that are traded and privately negotiated between two parties, without going through an exchange or intermediary, such as a clearinghouse. Exchange traded derivative contracts are those derivative instruments that are traded in specialized derivatives exchanges, such as futures or options exchanges. For further background on reform of the OTC derivatives markets, please see CRS Report R40965, *Key Issues in Derivatives Reform*, by Rena S. Miller; CRS Report R41398, *The Dodd-Frank Wall Street Reform and Consumer Protection Act: Title VII, Derivatives*, by Rena S. Miller and Kathleen Ann Ruane, CRS Report R40646, *Derivatives Regulation and Legislation Through the 111th Congress*, by Rena S. Miller, and CRS Report R42129, *Derivatives Legislation in the 112th Congress*, by Rena S. Miller.

[3] A credit default swap (CDS) is a credit derivative contract between two counterparties in which the buyer makes periodic payments to the seller and in return receives a sum of money if a certain credit event occurs (such as a default in an underlying financial instrument). Payoffs and collateral calls on CDSs issued on sub-prime mortgage collateral debt obligations (CDOs) were a primary cause of the problems of American International Group, Inc. (AIG) and other companies during the financial crisis. For more information on how a CDS works, see CRS Report RS22932, *Credit Default Swaps: Frequently Asked Questions*, by Edward V. Murphy and Rena S. Miller.

[4] Report of JPMorgan Chase & Co. Management Task Force, January 16, 2013. Available at: http://files.shareholder.com/downloads/ONE/2273002476x0x628656/4cb574a0-0bf5-4728-9582-625e4519b5ab/Task_Force_Report.pdf. For further details on the JP Morgan trading losses please see CRS Report R42665, *JP Morgan Trading Losses: Implications for the Volcker Rule and Other Regulation*, by Gary Shorter, Edward V. Murphy, and Rena S. Miller.

Group of Twenty (G-20)

The Group of Twenty, or G-20, is an informal forum for advancing international economic cooperation among 20 major advanced and emerging-market countries, consisting of the following members: Argentina, Australia, Brazil, Canada, China, France, Germany, India, Indonesia, Italy, Japan, Mexico, Russia, Saudi Arabia, South Africa, South Korea, Turkey, the United Kingdom, the United States, and the European Union. The G-20 was originally established in 1999 to facilitate discussions among G-20 finance ministers. The prominence of the G-20 increased with the onset of the global financial crisis in the fall of 2008, and the G-20 started meeting at the leader level, generally the political head of state. In September 2009, the G-20 leaders announced that, henceforth, the G-20 would be the "premier" forum for international economic cooperation. In its current form, the G-20 leaders meet annually, while finance ministers and central bank presidents meet in the Spring and the Fall prior to the annual leaders' meeting. On-going work of the G-20 is conducted by representatives of the national leaders, referred to as Sherpas. Russia assumed the Presidency of the G-20 on December 1, 2012, and will host the next meeting of G-20 leaders on September 5-6, 2013 in St. Petersburg.

According to standard finance theory, derivatives markets benefit financial markets and the wider economy by: improving the pricing of risk; adding to liquidity; and helping market participants manage their risks. In particular, derivatives are used by financial firms, corporations, farmers, and investors to hedge against, or speculate on, changes in prices, rates, or indices, or even on events such as the potential defaults on debts. As a result, they have added to liquidity and been instrumental in expanding financial opportunities for a broad range of market participants, particularly in mitigating risks associated with changes in exchange rates and interest rates. Nevertheless, OTC derivatives can add substantial risk to financial markets due to the very nature of derivatives. OTC derivatives contracts often involve lengthy commitments during which time a position can potentially generate a substantial counterparty credit exposure.[5] Also, since OTC derivatives often require a small initial outlay of cash, small changes in the value of the underlying securities of the derivatives can abruptly expand the potential liabilities and raise counterparty credit risk dramatically during periods of market turbulence.[6] In addition, derivatives markets and transactions span national borders and national regulators. Consequently, troubles in derivatives markets can reverberate far beyond the original source of the problem.

The Financial Crisis Inquiry Commission[7] concluded that derivatives contributed to the 2008-2009 financial crisis in three major ways. First, credit default swaps were instrumental in fueling the securitization of mortgages and mortgage-backed securities and in the subsequent housing bubble. Next credit default swaps were essential in creating synthetic collateralized debt obligations (CDO), or financial instruments that served as bets on the performance of real mortgage-backed securities, which amplified the losses from the collapse of the housing bubble by allowing multiple bets on the same securities and helped spread the losses throughout the financial system. Finally, once the housing boom ended, derivatives were at the center of the

---

[5] Vause, Nicholas, Counterparty Risk and Contract Volumes in the Credit Default Swap Market, *Quarterly Review*, Bank for International Settlements, December 2010, p. 59-61. Counterparty credit exposure, also known as counterparty risk, refers to the risk associated with the financial stability or creditworthiness of the party with whom one has entered into the OTC derivatives contract. Futures contracts, which are executed on exchanges, unlike OTC contracts, are guaranteed against default by the clearinghouse affiliated with the exchange.

[6] *82nd Annual Report*, Bank for International Settlements, Basel, June 24, 2012, p. 81. Available at: http://www.bis.org/publ/arpdf/ar2012e.pdf .

[7] The Financial Crimes Inquiry Commission was established in 2009 as part of the Fraud Enforcement and Recovery Act (P.L. 111-21) to examine the financial crisis in the United States. The Commission was comprised of a10-member panel of private citizens with experience in such areas as housing, economics, finance, market regulation, banking, and consumer protection. The Commission issued its final report in January 2011: *Financial Crisis Inquiry Report: Final Report of the National Commission on the Causes of the Financial and Economic Crisis in the United States*, Financial Crimes Inquiry Commission, January 2011, p. xxiv-xxv.

---

crisis due to: 1) concerns that losses associated with derivatives would trigger cascading losses throughout the global financial system; and 2) the lack of transparency concerning the overall size of the derivatives market and the extent of derivatives transactions between systemically important financial institutions that directly added to uncertainty and panic in global financial markets.

Perhaps the best known example of problems stemming from large OTC derivatives exposure in the financial crisis came from the near-collapse of the large conglomerate American International Group, Inc. (AIG), which wrote about $1.8 trillion worth of OTC derivatives contracts for credit default swaps. These credit default swaps guaranteed payment if certain mortgage-backed securities defaulted or experienced other "credit events." Many of AIG's contracts did require it to post collateral[8] as the credit quality of the underlying securities (or AIG's own credit rating) deteriorated, but AIG did not post an initial margin,[9] as this was deemed unnecessary because of the firm's triple-A rating. As the subprime crisis worsened, AIG was subjected to margin calls that it could not meet. To avert bankruptcy, with the risk of global financial chaos, the Federal Reserve and the Treasury put tens of billions of dollars into AIG, the bulk of which went to its derivatives counterparties.

The AIG case illustrates two aspects of OTC markets that are central to derivatives reform proposals. First, as noted above, AIG was able to amass an OTC derivatives position so large that it threatened to destabilize the entire financial system when the firm suffered unexpected losses, and the risks of default to AIG derivatives counterparties grew. In a market with mandatory clearing and margin, in which AIG would have been required to post an initial margin to cover potential losses, there is a stronger possibility that AIG would have run out of money long before the size of its position had reached $1.8 trillion.

Second, because OTC contracts were not reported to regulators, the U.S. Federal Reserve (the Fed) and the U.S. Treasury Department lacked information about which institutions were exposed to AIG, and the size of those exposures. Uncertainty among market participants about the size and distribution of potential derivatives losses flowing from the failure of a major dealer was a factor that exacerbated the "freezing" of credit markets during the peaks of the crisis, and made banks unwilling to lend to each other.

A basic theme in derivatives reform proposals is to get the OTC market to act more like the exchange-traded futures market—in particular, to have bilateral OTC swaps cleared by a third-party clearing organization.

Generally, OTC derivatives are used in a variety of ways, including hedging, investing, exploiting arbitrage opportunities, and position-taking. OTC derivative instruments are generally referred to

---

[8] Posting collateral refers to pledging assets as security for the value of a loan, or in the case of derivatives trades, to cover potential losses.

[9] Margin refers to the amount of money or collateral deposited by a customer with his broker. Initial margin is the amount of margin required by the broker when a futures position is opened. The terms "collateral" and "margin" are similar—both are forms of a downpayment against potential losses to guard against a counterparty's nonpayment—but technically they are not interchangeable. A margining agreement requires that cash or very liquid securities be deposited immediately with the counterparty. After this initial deposit, margin accounts are marked-to-market, usually daily. In the event of default, the counterparty holding the margin can liquidate the margin account. By contrast, collateral arrangements usually allow a wider range of assets than what is allowed as margin. Also, settlement of collateral shortfalls tends to be less frequent than under margining arrangements.

as swaps. Yet swaps have widely differing characteristics and degrees of standardization, and can include bets on a number of different types of assets. The global OTC derivatives markets are dominated by five different types of swaps: foreign exchange swaps; interest rate swaps; equity-linked swaps; commodity swaps; and credit default swaps, as indicated in **Table 1**. At the end of 2011, the total notional amounts outstanding of OTC derivatives amounted to $647.8 trillion, down about 8% from the $706.9 trillion in derivatives recorded in June 2011. The notional amount, also called the reference amount, refers to the underlying value of the assets that are being bet on through a derivatives contract. **Figure 1** depicts the relative total sizes of the global derivatives market; world assets; world GDP; and the world's official reserves. It demonstrates that the size of the global derivatives market, in terms of notional value, tends to dwarf these other major categories.

Table 1. Global OTC Derivatives Markets

(amounts outstanding, in trillions of U.S. dollars)

	Notional Amounts Outstanding				Gross Market Value			
	June 2010	Dec. 2010	June 2011	Dec. 2011	June 2010	Dec. 2010	June 2011	Dec. 2011
Grand Total	$582.7	$601.0	$706.9	$647.8	$24.7	$21.3	$19.5	$27.3
Foreign Exchange Contracts	53.1	57.8	64.7	63.3	2.5	2.5	2.3	2.6
Interest Rate Contracts	451.8	465.3	553.2	504.1	17.5	14.7	13.2	20.0
Equity-linked Contracts	6.3	5.6	6.8	6.0	0.7	0.6	0.7	0.7
Commodity Contracts	2.9	2.9	3.2	3.1	0.5	0.5	0.5	0.5
Credit-Default Swaps	30.3	39.5	46.5	42.6	1.8	1.5	1.4	2.0

Source: *Quarterly Review*, Table 19, Bank for International Settlements, June 2012.

Note: The notional amount of OTC derivatives is defined as the gross nominal amount of the underlying assets of all OTC derivatives deals concluded but not yet settled. The notional amount provides a measure of the total market size, but does not represent the amounts that are actually at risk. Gross market value represents the sum of the absolute values of all open contracts, or the replacement cost of the contracts themselves, but not of the underlying assets. Thus, gross market value is usually smaller than notional amounts outstanding, but some argue that it represents a better estimate of the actual amount of money at risk through derivatives transactions.

Figure 1. Relative Size of Global Derivatives Market

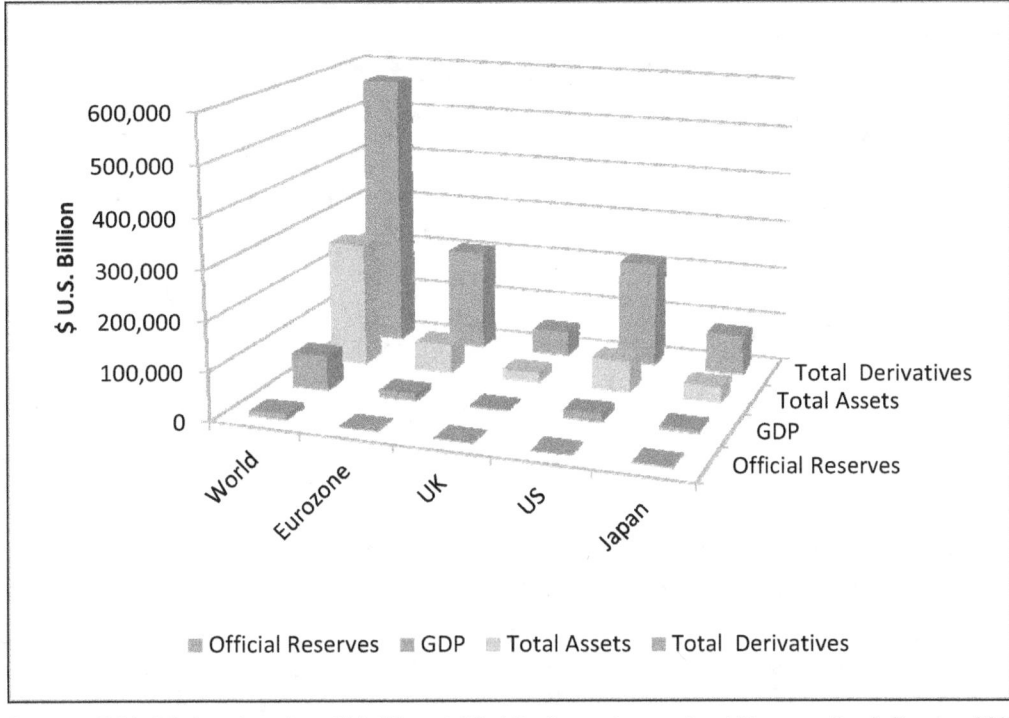

Source: Table 2 below, based on *Global Financial Stability Report*, International Monetary Fund, October 2012. Statistical Appendix, Table 1; *Quarterly Review*, Bank for International Settlements, September, 2012, Tables 20b and 21b.

Derivatives and Global Capital Markets

Financial markets that trade derivatives grew rapidly over the past decade and now serve large trades involving vast amounts of funds, as indicated in **Table 2**. According to data published by the International Monetary Fund (IMF) and the Bank for International Settlements (BIS), global trading in OTC foreign exchange derivatives and OTC interest rate derivatives amounted to $567 trillion in 2011, or approximately nine times world gross domestic product (GDP) of $70 trillion. These data do not include trading in equity and commodity-linked derivatives, which likely would boost these numbers substantially higher. In addition, the total notional value, or the total gross nominal value of the underlying assets, of derivatives in 2011 was reported as being more than twice the size of the total value of all stocks, bonds, and bank assets, as indicated in **Table 2**. The United States, with the largest gross domestic product (GDP) of any country (and about the same size as the EU's GDP) also had the largest single share of OTC interest and exchange rate derivatives trading in 2011 – a share slightly greater than that of the Euro area -- in terms of the notional value of the derivatives.

Table 2. Selected Indicators of the Size of the Global Capital Markets, 2011

(in billions of U.S. dollars)

	Gross Domestic Product (GDP)	Total Official Reserves	Bonds, Equities, and Bank Assets				OTC Derivatives		
			Total	Stock Market Capitalization	Debt Securities	Bank Assets	Total	OTC Foreign Exchange Derivatives	OTC Interest Rate Derivatives
World	$69,899	10,650	255,855	47,089	98,388	110,378	567,447	63,349	504,098
European Union	16,426	468	82,251	8,530	31,548	42,172	NA	NA	NA
Euro Area	13,118	316	58,874	4,586	24,976	29,311	207,937	23,235	184,702
United Kingdom	2,431	79	19,055	3,266	4,839	10,950	50,390	7,023	43,367
United States	15,076	137	63,976	15,640	33,700	14,635	215,925	54,061	161,864
Japan	5,866	1,258	31,666	3,540	15,369	12,756	80,480	13,661	66,819
Emerging markets	25,438	6,944	44,553	9,771	9,240	25,542	NA	NA	NA

Source: *Global Financial Stability Report*, International Monetary Fund, October 2012. Statistical Appendix, Table 1; *Quarterly Review*, Bank for International Settlements, September, 2012, Tables 20b and 21b.

Note: Total derivatives do not include equity and commodity-linked derivatives. Total OTC derivatives refers to total notional amount outstanding, as of end-December 2011, based on BIS statistics.

G-20 Efforts to Reform OTC Derivatives Markets

The financial crisis of 2008-2009 exposed weaknesses in the OTC markets that contributed to the build-up of systemic risk and threatened to disrupt the functioning of international financial markets. OTC derivatives are traded by a large and diverse group of market participants, including banks, hedge funds, pension funds, other institutional investors, corporations, and government entities. This market, however, is dominated by a limited number of dealers. Such dealers provide liquidity to the market by selling derivatives contracts to customers and managing the resulting risk exposures through offsetting transactions in the underlying assets, exchange traded derivatives, and further trades with dealers and traders in OTC markets. These dealers are highly interconnected through a network of trades and, therefore, are highly exposed to spillover, or contagion, effects from turmoil in other parts of the markets. Such market disruptions can trigger a chain of credit-related losses which, in turn, could result in severe market disruptions and potentially a chain of defaults.[10] According to the Financial Stability Board (FSB),[11] these weaknesses include: 1) the build-up of large counterparty exposures between particular market participants through collateralized debt obligations[12] (CDOs) and credit default swaps which have

---

[10] *Implementing OTC Derivatives Market Reforms*, Financial Stability Board, October 25, 2010, p. 9. Available at: http://www.financialstabilityboard.org/publications/r_101025.pdf.

[11] Ibid, p. 8.

[12] Collateralized debt obligations (CDOs) are a type of structured asset-backed security whose value and payments are derived from a portfolio of fixed-income underlying assets. CDOs based on sub-prime mortgages were at the heart of (continued...)

---

not been appropriately risk-managed; 2) contagion risk arising from the interconnectedness of the OTC derivatives market participants; and 3) the limited transparency of overall counterparty credit risk exposures that can precipitate a loss of confidence and market liquidity in times of stress.

Financial Stability Board (FSB)

The Financial Stability Board (FSB) was created at the G-20 London Summit in April 2009 as the successor to the Financial Stability Forum. The mission of the group is to coordinate and monitor at the international level the work of national financial authorities and international standard-setting bodies, in the interest of financial stability. The FSB is chaired by Mark Carney, Governor of the Bank of Canada; its Secretariat is hosted by the Bank for International Settlements in Basel, Switzerland. The United States is represented at the FSB by the Department of Treasury, the Board of Governors of the Federal Reserve System, and the Securities and Exchange Commission. Members of the FSB include: Argentina, Australia, Brazil, Canada, China, France, Germany, Hong Kong, India, Indonesia, Italy, Japan, Mexico, the Netherlands, Russia, South Korea, Saudi Arabia, Singapore, South Africa, Spain, Switzerland, Turkey, the United Kingdom, the United States, and such international organizations as the Bank for International Settlements, European Central Bank, European Commission, International Monetary Fund, Organization for Economic Cooperation and Development, World Bank, Basel Committee on Banking Supervision (BCBS), Committee on the Global Financial System (CGFS), Committee on Payment and Settlement Systems (CPSS), International Association of Insurance Supervisors (IAIS), International Accounting Standards Board (IASB), and the International Organization of Securities Commissions (IOSCO). For further information please see http://www.financialstabilityboard.org/.

In November 2008, as the heads of state of the G-20 nations met in Washington DC to respond to the financial crisis, they agreed to implement a number of reforms[13] to address the perceived failures in the financial system. The G-20 leaders concluded at that time that major failures in regulation and supervision of financial markets, in combination with increased risk-taking by banks, had created fragilities that threatened to undermine the financial system. In particular, the leaders concluded that the global financial system had become highly interconnected, but that the system lacked a commensurate level of transparency regarding the associated counterparty exposures that was comparable to the level of complexity. The growing interconnectedness of financial markets means that a shock that originates in one country or asset market can quickly affect other markets and other countries, known as contagion.

However, while global financial markets have become increasingly interconnected, large and highly complex financial firms have grown to straddle continents and markets. At the same time, regulators and regulations have remained national in scope and have been unprepared to address

---

(...continued)

the 2008-2009 global financial crises. CDOs are assigned different risk classes or tranches, with "senior" tranches considered to be the safest. Since interest and principal payments are made in order of seniority, junior tranches offer higher coupon payments (and interest rates) or lower prices to compensate for additional default risk. Investors, pension funds, and insurance companies buy CDOs.

[13] In addition to reforms in the over-the-counter derivatives market, the G-20 leaders agreed to make reforms in the following areas: 1) improving the quality and quantity of bank capital and liquidity through reforms known as Basel III; 2) addressing systemically important financial institutions through resolution frameworks, higher loss absorbency, and more intensive supervisory oversight; 3) developing concepts for greater supervision or regulation of the shadow banking system, or financial intermediaries that conduct maturity, credit, and liquidity transformation without explicit access to central bank liquidity or public sector credit guarantees; 4) developing and adopting macroprudential policy tools and frameworks (see: *Macroprudential Policy Tools and Frameworks: Update to G-20 Finance Ministers and Central Bank Governors,* Financial Stability Board, February 14, 2011); 5) strengthening accounting standards; 6) identifying and examining financial stability issues that are relevant for emerging and developing economies; 7) exploring options to protect consumer finance; 8) reducing reliance on credit rating agencies; 9) addressing gaps in data revealed by the financial crisis; and 10) developing recommendations to promote market integrity and efficiency to mitigate risks posed by technological developments. See: http://www.imf.org/external/np/g20/pdf/021411.pdf.

financial crises with cross-border implications. Due to the challenges of effectively harmonizing all regulations across national boundaries and legal systems, and possibly as a result of few effective institutional mechanisms to ensure such coordination of national regulatory bodies, national regulators have focused on meeting national objectives. At times, this can lead to a lack of uniformity, or even conflicts, between regulatory regimes. Arguably, it can lead to national priorities subsuming concerns about global financial stability.

Through successive summits, G-20 leaders have addressed these perceived failures by refining their goals and developing increasingly detailed objectives for the G-20 members to improve financial market infrastructures (FMIs).[14] One of these first steps included "improving the infrastructure of over-the-counter" (OTC) derivative markets and credit default swaps.[15] The Bank for International Settlements (BIS) has argued that providing harmonized standards for FMIs is important to the functioning of the financial system and in fostering stability. The BIS concluded that FMIs, or systemically important payments systems, play a critical role in the financial system and the broader economy by "facilitating the clearing, settlement, and recording of monetary and other financial transactions, such as payments, securities, and derivatives contracts....While safe and efficient FMIs contribute to maintaining and promoting financial stability and economic growth, FMIs also concentrate risk. If not properly managed, FMIs can be sources of financial shocks, such as liquidity dislocations and credit losses, or a major channel through which these shocks are transmitted across domestic and international financial markets."[16]

In addition, at the November 2008 Washington DC summit, the leaders supported actions by regulators to speed up efforts to reduce the systemic risks associated with credit default swaps and over-the-counter derivatives transactions. They also supported efforts to ensure greater transparency for OTC derivatives and an adequate infrastructure to support the growing volumes of OTC derivatives trading.[17] These three objectives – improving transparency, mitigating risk, and protecting against market abuse – continue to drive G-20 reforms of the OTC derivatives markets.

The G-20 leaders have expressed their support for reforming the OTC derivatives markets in successive G-20 summits. Actions taken by the G-20 leaders at some of the Summits have been particularly noteworthy:

---

[14] Financial market infrastructures (FMIs) are generally viewed as systemically important multilateral payment systems among participating institutions that facilitate the clearing, settlement, and recording of monetary and other financial transactions, such as payments, securities, and derivatives contracts. According to the Bank for International Settlements, FMIs provide participants with centralized clearing, settlement, and recording of financial transactions among themselves or between each of them and a central party to allow for greater efficiency and reduced costs and risks. Some FMIs are critical in helping central banks conduct monetary policy and maintain financial stability. See: *Principles for Financial Market Infrastructures*, Bank for International Settlements, April 2012. Available at: http://www.bis.org/publ/cpss101a.pdf.

[15] *Declaration of the Summit on Financial Markets and the World Economy*, G-20, November 15, 2008, available at: http://www.un.org/ga/president/63/commission/declarationG-20.pdf. For further background on credit default swaps as derivative instruments and their related issues, please see CRS Report RS22932, *Credit Default Swaps: Frequently Asked Questions*, by Edward V. Murphy and Rena S. Miller.

[16] *Principles for Financial Market Infrastructures*, p. 5.

[17] See: *Declaration of the Summit on Financial Markets and the World Economy*, G-20, November 15, 2008, p. 7. Available at: http://georgewbush-whitehouse.archives.gov/news/releases/2008/11/20081115-1.html.

- At the Pittsburgh Summit in September 2009, G-20 leaders agreed that all standardized OTC derivative contracts[18] should be traded on exchanges or electronic trading platforms, where appropriate, and cleared through central counterparties[19] (CCPs) by the end of 2012.[20] In addition, they agreed that all OTC contracts should be reported to trade repositories (TRs).[21] The G-20 leaders also tasked the Financial Stability Board with assessing the implementation of the agreed reforms and determining whether those reforms would be sufficient to achieve the main goal of improving transparency in the derivatives markets, mitigating systemic risk, and protecting against market abuse.

- In October 2010, the FSB published a report containing 21 recommendations for the G-20 nations to assist them in implementing the G-20 leaders' commitments concerning standardization, central clearing, exchange or electronic platform trading, and reporting of OTC derivatives transactions to trade repositories.[22] The FSB then published an updated report in October 2011, a third report in June 2012,[23] and a fourth report in October 2012.[24] These reports detail country commitments in six specific areas of reform: 1) standardization of OTC derivatives contracts; 2) central clearing of OTC derivatives contracts; 3) exchange or electronic platform trading; 4) transparency and trading; 5) reporting to trade repositories; and 6) application of central clearing requirements. In April 2011, the Committee on Payments and Settlement Systems of the Bank for International Settlements published a consultative report on recommendations

---

[18] According to the FSB, in determining whether a contract is "standardized" and, therefore, one that is suitable for central clearing, authorities should consider: 1) the degree of standardization of a product's contractual terms and operational processes; 2) the depth and liquidity of the market for the product; and 3) the availability of fair, reliable and generally accepted pricing sources. See: *Implementing OTC Derivatives Market Reform*, Financial Stability Board, October 25, 2010. Available at: http://www.financialstabilityboard.org/publications/r_101025.pdf.

[19] Central counterparties (CCPs) interpose themselves as intermediaries between counterparties to contracts traded in one or more financial markets. Instead of a buyer and seller interacting directly, in a central counterparty system, the central counterparty acts as the buyer to every seller and the seller to every buyer, through a system known as novation, thereby ensuring the performance of open contracts. Novation is an open-offer system of legally binding contracts. CCPs generally attempt to reduce risks to participants by requiring the participants to provide collateral to cover current and potential future exposures.

[20] G-20 Leaders Statement: The Pittsburgh Summit, September 24-25, 2009, p. 8. Available at: http://www.G-20.utoronto.ca/2009/2009communique0925.html.

[21] A trade repository is an entity that maintains a centralized electronic record of transaction data. Timely and reliable access to data stored in trade repositories potentially can enhance the transparency of transaction information to relevant authorities and the public to identify and evaluate the potential risks posed to the broader financial system, promote financial stability, and support the detection and prevention of market abuse.

[22] *Implementing OTC Derivatives Market Reforms*, Financial Stability Board, October 25, 2010. Available at: http://www.financialstabilityboard.org/publications/r_101025.pdf.

[23] *OTC Derivatives Market Reforms: Third Progress Report on Implementation*, Financial Stability Board, June 15, 2012. See http://www.financialstabilityboard.org/publications/r_120615.pdf.

[24] *OTC Derivatives Market Reforms: Fourth Progress Report on Implementation*, Financial Stability Board, October 31, 2012. See https://www.financialstabilityboard.org/publications/r_121031a.pdf.

---

regarding OTC derivatives data reporting.[25] In January 2012, the Committee published its final report.[26]

- At the Cannes G-20 Summit in November 2011, the leaders adopted the recommendations of the derivatives markets working group and agreed to continue making progress in reforming the OTC derivatives market. The summit final communiqué declared that:

    Reforming the over-the-counter derivatives markets is crucial to building a more resilient financial system. All standardized over-the-counter derivatives contracts should be traded on exchanges or electronic trading platforms, where appropriate, and centrally cleared, by the end of 2012; OTC derivatives contracts should be reported to trade repositories, and non-centrally cleared contracts should be subject to higher capital requirements. We agree to cooperate further to avoid loopholes and overlapping regulations. A coordination group is being established by the FSB to address some of these issues, complementing the existing OTC derivatives working group.[27]

Assessing G-20 Derivatives Market Reforms

As indicated above, the FSB was tasked by the G-20 with monitoring and reporting on the success of G-20 nations in meeting the year-end 2012 deadline of implementing the OTC derivatives market reforms. These reforms have focused on the three major objectives of the reforms as articulated by the G-20 leaders at the Washington, DC summit: improving transparency, mitigating risk, and protecting against market abuse. These three objectives have been addressed through five broad areas of reforms: 1) standardizing OTC derivatives contracts; 2) developing international standards and policy for central clearing and for risk management of non-centrally cleared derivatives; 3) developing international standards and policy for exchanges or electronic platform trading; 4) developing the infrastructure to facilitate reporting OTC transactions to trade repositories (TR); and 5) developing and implement international standards and policies for capital requirements.

As a result of self-assessments by G-20 members, except for France, Germany, and Italy, which are represented by the EU in the survey, and such FSB members as Singapore and Switzerland, the FSB offered four general conclusions:

- Only Japan and the United States had adopted the necessary legislation to reach the goal of having derivatives centrally cleared by the end of 2012, while the EU had reached a political consensus regarding legislation. Most authorities estimated that a significant proportion of interest rate derivatives will be centrally cleared by year-end 2012, but they were less confident of progress for other asset

---

[25] *Report on OTC Derivatives Data Reporting and Aggregation Requirements: Consultative Report*, Committee on Payment and Settlement Systems, August 2011. See http://www.bis.org/publ/cpss96.pdf.

[26] *Report on OTC Derivatives Data Reporting and Aggregation Requirements: Final Report*, Committee on Payment and Settlement Systems, January 2012. See http://www.bis.org/publ/cpss100.htm.

[27] *Cannes Summit Final Declaration*, November 4, 2011, par 24. Available at: http://www.G-20.utoronto.ca/2011/2011-cannes-declaration-111104-en.html.

classes and could not make firm estimates when central clearing could be achieved.[28]

- On the whole, the countries surveyed were markedly behind in implementing commitments that standardized contracts should be traded on exchanges or electronic platforms by year-end 2012. According to the BIS, increasing the proportion of the market traded on organized platforms is important for improving transparency, mitigating systemic risk, and protecting against market abuse. Only the United States had passed legislation with requirements for pre- and post-trade transparency and proposed detailed regulations; the EU had made legislative proposals, and the Japanese Diet had approved legislation with provisions to improve the transparency of derivatives markets.[29]

- The increased standardization of contracts is a core element of the G-20 nations' commitment relating to central clearing, organized trading and reporting to TRs, and increasing the benefits in terms of improved transparency, reduced systemic risk, and greater protection against market abuse.[30] Most countries have made progress in developing legislative frameworks to have all OTC derivatives contracts reported to trade repositories (TRs), although not all members have adopted legislation. The majority of members have published consultative documents regarding the establishment of TRs and the related reporting requirements.

- The FSB lacked information on capital requirements for non-bank regulated entities, because capital standards related to banks' exposures to central clearing parties are still being developed. The Basel Committee on Banking Supervision (BCBS) published a report[31] in November 2011 on capital standards for banks' exposures and the BIS published a report[32] in March 2012 on collateral requirements for central clearing of OTC derivatives and a report in July 2012 on capital requirements for bank exposures to central counterparties.[33] The BIS expected that by the start of 2012 the higher capital requirements associated with the higher counterparty credit risk of non-centrally cleared derivatives contracts would have been met internationally for banks through the Basel III standards. The BIS expects that the higher capital standards for non-centrally cleared contracts will provide incentives for standardization and central clearing.

In March 2010, 14 of the largest derivatives dealers[34] committed to take a number of steps to make derivatives trading more transparent, expand central clearing, improve standardization of

---

[28] *OTC Derivatives Market Reforms: Fourth Progress Report,* p. 3.

[29] *Ibid.,* p. 4.

[30] *Ibid.,* p. 5.

[31] *Capitalization of Bank Exposures to Central Counterparties: Consultative Document*, Basel Committee on Banking Supervision, November 2011.

[32] *Collateral Requirements for Mandatory Central Clearing of Over-the-Counter Derivatives*, BIS Working Papers No. 373, Bank for International Settlements, March 2012.

[33] *Capital Requirements for Bank Exposures to Central Counterparties*, Bank for International Settlements, July 2012. For a bank that acts as a clearing member of a CCP for its own purposes, the requirements stipulate that the bank apply a risk weight of 2% to its exposure to the central counterparty.

[34] The 14 dealers who were signatories included: Bank of America Corp., Barclays Capital, BNP Paribas, Citigroup Inc., Credit Suisse, Deutsche Bank, Goldman Sachs Group Inc., HSBC, JP Morgan Chase, Morgan Stanley, RBS, (continued...)

---

derivatives contracts, and manage collateral associated with derivatives trading.[35] These commitments included specific target levels for the central clearing of OTC credit derivatives and OTC interest rate derivatives that were eligible for central clearing counterparties. It was acknowledged, however, that the enhanced clearing targets covered only part of the OTC market, because most derivative contracts were not eligible for central counterparty clearing. In order to address this issue and to implement the G-20 recommendations, the FSB initiated a working group,[36] led by the Committee on Payment and Settlement Systems (CPSS) of the Bank for International Settlements (BIS), the International Organization of Securities Commissions (IOSCO), and the European Commission (EC) to assess and develop policy options for promoting the increased use of standardized products and for implementing at the global level the mandatory clearing of derivatives contracts and the exchange or electronic trading requirements.

The following sections examine the major issues involved and the progress made to date in the five broad areas of reforms addressed by the FSB surveys: 1) standards for OTC derivatives contracts; 2) central clearing and non-centrally cleared derivatives; 3) exchanges or electronic platform trading; 4) reporting to trade repositories (TR); and 5) capital requirements.

Progress in Standardizing OTC Derivatives Contracts

Issue: Standardization of derivative contracts is a core element in meeting the G-20 commitments for central clearing, organized trading, and reporting to trade repositories (TRs). As indicated previously, 14 major derivatives dealers developed a broad "roadmap" for increasing standardization of derivatives products. In a second, 2011 letter to New York Federal Reserve President William C. Dudley, the group discussed this roadmap, consisting of three core initiatives to: 1) develop ongoing analyses to benchmark the level of standardization in each asset class; 2) continue on going work in standardizing products in each asset class; and 3) work with central clearing parties, trade repositories, and other infrastructure providers to standardize processes in each asset class.[37]

Progress: According to the FSB, about half of the surveyed countries have adopted, or have plans to adopt, legislative and regulatory measures to increase the use of standardized derivative products and processes. Those jurisdictions with markets that already are highly standardized reported that they expected to remain at those levels.

Latest Developments: The October 2012 FSB progress report concluded that uncertainty over the legislative and regulatory requirements about which specific products and market participants will be covered under new clearing requirements is slowing progress in offering products for clearing and in developing new services to support mandatory central clearing. The FSB also indicated that the lack of standardization of financial products and uncertainty about which

---

(...continued)

Societe Generale, UBS, and Wells Fargo. In addition to the large derivatives dealers, the letter was signed by large "buy-side" users of OTC derivatives, such as funds, and their trade groups. See Letter to Honorable William C. Dudley, President, Federal Reserve Bank of New York, March 1, 2010, available at: http://www.newyorkfed.org/newsevents/news/markets/2010/100301_letter.pdf.

[35] *Ibid.*

[36] Called the FSB's OTC Derivatives Working Group (ODWG).

[37] Second Letter to William C. Dudley, dated March 31, 2011, available at: http://www.newyorkfed.org/newsevents/news/markets/2011/SCL0331.pdf.

features will ultimately be used as the measure for "standardization" across jurisdictions is slowing progress in offering new products and services.[38]

Progress in Developing International Standards for Clearing and Risk Management for Uncleared Derivatives

Issue. The mandatory clearing of standardized derivatives through central counterparties (CCPs) such as clearinghouses stands as the centerpiece of international efforts to improve stability in global financial markets, as it is expected to enhance counterparty risk management. According to recent research, an expanded role for CCPs fills a number of important market roles, as described by the European Central Bank (ECB).[39] First, CCPs are in a unique position to assess the risks that are faced by the financial system as a whole, because they have information on all cleared transactions. Such information enhances transparency and improves the ability of CCPs to assess the risks to existing transactions that may arise from new transactions. Second, since CCPs have a more complete understanding of risk exposures than individual counterparties, they can provide a more accurate assessment of exposures, which improves risk management and the allocation of capital. Third, as independent clearing agents, CCPs have the ability to provide effective insurance against counterparty risk by pooling risks.

The growing role of CCPs also entails certain risks. CCPs are arguably systemically important institutions that could become "too big to fail." According to some analysts, this potential for systemic risk argues in favor of the regulation, supervision, and oversight of CCPs.[40] In addition, effectively implementing central clearing is affected by such factors as: the size of the market; governance of the market; and the structure of the market. Since pooling risk by a CCP is one of the main benefits of centralized clearing, the size and liquidity of the market is important. Achieving sufficient liquidity may require mandatory central clearing of transactions. Relying on market incentives alone may not be enough to induce individual participants to join in central clearing, because the costs of clearing for an individual participant may outweigh the benefits. The economic benefits of central clearing tend to be fully realized only as the number of participants rises.[41]

The ECB also contends that CCPs require outside supervision to ensure that the profit motive of the CCPs does not conflict with the requirement for providing appropriate risk mitigation. In addition, supervising CCPs requires balancing efficiency with safety considerations. Competition between CCPs may decentralize the clearing process, making the process efficient, but having it operate at a level that is less than optimal. On the other hand, concentrated clearing may increase the risks of concentrating excessive risk and present obstacles to adequately overseeing and supervising CCPs, especially for CCPs that operate on a cross-border basis.[42]

---

[38] *OTC Derivatives Market Reforms, Fourth Progress Report*, p. 24.

[39] *Financial Stability Review*, European Central Bank, December 2012, pp. 98-100.

[40] For more on this policy debate please see e.g. Darrell Duffie and Haoxiang Zhu , "Does a Central Clearing Counterparty Reduce Counterparty Risk?" at http://www.mit.edu/~zhuh/DuffieZhu_CCP.pdf; and see also European Central Bank. 2009. Credit Default Swaps and Counterparty Risk. European Central Bank, Financial Stability and Supervision. See also IOSCO, "Recommendations for Central Counterparties," (2004) at http://www.bis.org/publ/cpss61.pdf.

[41] *Financial Stability Review*, December 2012, p. 99.

[42] *Ibid*, p. 100.

Based on recommendations prepared by the International Organization of Securities Commissions (IOSCO)[43] and the Committee on Payment and Settlement Systems (CPSS), [44] the BIS proposed a set of standards for the central clearing of derivatives that was adopted by the G-20 members and some FSB members in 2012. According to the FSB, these standards harmonize, strengthen, and replace previously separate sets of international principles for financial market infrastructures. In addition, the standards "seek to enhance safety and efficiency in payment, clearing, settlement and recording arrangements and, more broadly, to limit systemic risk and foster transparency and financial stability."[45]

According to the BIS, the "nature of counterparty exposures in OTC derivatives markets is widely considered to have exacerbated" the 2008-2009 financial crisis and "that exposures were often inadequately collateralized." The BIS also concluded that: "[C]learing trades centrally can mitigate these structural weaknesses."[46] About half of all derivatives contracts are not cleared by a CCP, but are simply settled as bilateral contracts. This has arguably resulted in a proliferation of redundant overlapping contracts, exacerbating counterparty risks and adding to the complexity and opacity of the interconnections in the financial system.[47]

CCPs are expected to reduce counterparty credit risk by: 1) imposing multilateral netting of exposures whereby market participants net all of their derivative positions with a common counterparty; and 2) reducing risk by enforcing collateralization of exposures. The G-20 leaders agreed that all standardized derivatives contracts should be cleared through central counterparties by the end of 2012 to help mitigate systemic risk. That potentially means a sharp increase in the volume of transactions and in the collateral requirements of central counterparties.[48] Non-centrally cleared contracts should be subject to higher capital requirements, according to the Basel Committee on Banking Supervision.[49] These standards also include measures for evaluating the factors that should be taken into account when determining whether a derivative contract is standardized and, therefore, suitable for clearing. According to 2012 data used by the FSB, 40% of interest rate derivatives were cleared through a central counterparty (CCP); but only about 10% of credit default swaps were cleared by a CCP. [50] Except for the United States, few of the G-20 nations were confident that significant proportions of credit or commodity derivatives would be centrally cleared by year-end 2012, and no G-20 country indicated that large proportions of equity or foreign exchange derivatives would be centrally cleared by year-end 2012.[51]

---

[43] *Requirements for Mandatory Clearing*, Technical Committee of the International Organization of Securities Commissions, February 2012.

[44] *Principles for Financial Market Infrastructures*, Bank for International Settlements, Committee on Payment and Settlement Systems and the Technical Committee of the International Organization of Securities Commissions, April 2012.

[45] *OTC Derivatives Market Reforms: Third Progress Report,* p. 11.

[46] Heller, Daniel, and Nicholas Vause, Expansion of Central Clearing, *BIS Quarterly Review*, June 2011. Available at: http://www.bis.org/publ/qtrpdf/r_qt1106.htm.

[47] Making Over-The-Counter Derivatives Safer: The Role of Central Counterparties, *Global Financial Stability Report*, International Monetary Fund, April 2010. Available at:http://www.imf.org/external/pubs/ft/gfsr/2010/01/pdf/chap3.pdf.

[48] Heller, Daniel, and Nicholas Vause, Collateral Requirements for Mandatory Central Clearing of Over-the-Counter Derivatives, *BIS Working Papers* No. 373, Bank for International Settlements, March 2012. Available at: http://www.bis.org/publ/work373.pdf.

[49] *Margining Requirements for Non-Centrally Cleared Derivatives*, Bank for International Settlements, Basel Committee on Banking Supervision, July 2012. Available at: http://www.bis.org/publ/bcbs226.pdf.

[50] *OTC Derivatives Market Reforms: Fourth Report,* p. 18.

[51] *OTC Derivatives Market Reforms: Third Progress Report*, p. 14-15.

Progress. The FSB's October 2012 report indicated that the EU, Japan, Hong Kong, and the United States had taken significant steps towards implementing legislation that mandates central clearing of standardized OTC derivatives. Other jurisdictions were generally less advanced, but reported making progress.[52] Also, the FSB noted that in many jurisdictions, including the United States, Japan, and the EU, legislative changes must be followed up with more technical implementing regulations in order for the requirements to become fully effective. Some jurisdictions have been waiting for the key elements of the regulatory frameworks adopted in the United States, Japan and the EU before adopting their own regulations. According to the FSB, the basic market infrastructure is in place and "does not appear to be an impediment to further progress in meeting the G-20 commitments for OTC derivatives trading, central clearing, and reporting."[53] The FSB also concluded that regulatory uncertainty remains the "most significant impediment to further progress and to comprehensive use of market infrastructure." As a result, it urged jurisdictions to promptly put in place their legislation and regulations.

According to the FSB, most of the jurisdictions in the G-20 countries require CCPs to register or obtain an exemption from registration from the relevant domestic regulators in that jurisdiction in order to provide clearing services to its domestic market participants. This registration requirement applies both where the CCP has a local presence and where it offers cross-border services, which means that CCPs intending to offer services in multiple locations are required to register in multiple jurisdictions in order to provide services to market participants operating in those jurisdictions. These requirements are being felt by some of the largest banks and brokerage firms in the world, with subsidiaries, affiliates, or branches in multiple jurisdictions that serve as clearing members of CCPs.[54]

Latest Developments. In October 2012, the FSB reported a number of conclusions following a survey of the G-20 members on the extent and progress of meeting the year-end 2012 goal of broad-based central clearing of derivatives contracts. The main FSB conclusions are:

1. CCPs are available to clear some OTC derivatives products in each of the five asset classes (foreign exchange contracts; interest rate contracts; equity-linked contracts; commodity contracts; and credit default swaps), with many of the CCPs expected to expand clearing services in the near term.

2. Of the nineteen CCPs included in the FSB's survey, nine are located in different jurisdictions; five reported offering services across borders and being registered in multiple jurisdictions, while 13 were supervised in and offered services in the same jurisdiction in which they are located.

3. CCPs apply their membership criteria to applicants located domestically and abroad, but direct clearing members generally are located in the same jurisdiction as the CCP.

4. Timelines for clearing new products vary considerably based on the complexity of the product; in some cases, CCPs were unable to estimate the time for introducing new products because of variation in risk management procedures and regulatory approvals.

---

[52] *OTC Derivatives Market Reforms: Fourth Progress Report,* p. 7.

[53] *Ibid,* p. 1.

[54] *Ibid,* p. 21.

5. Approximately half of the CCPs reported operational links to other types of market infrastructure, most commonly organized trading platforms and other CCPs.

The FSB also published in November 2012 the results[55] of a survey concerning approaches the G-20 and FSB countries expect to take on central clearing. The survey asked the countries whether their approach to central clearing would be based on the use of domestic clearing infrastructure or infrastructure located in other jurisdictions, and whether they would impose mandatory clearing requirements or rely on economic incentives, or some combination of both. According to the FSB survey, the majority of countries indicated that market participants would be able to use either domestic or cross-border CCPs to clear OTC derivatives contracts, while some countries indicated that market participants would use domestic CCPs only due to characteristics specific to a particular domestic market. In addition, the FSB concluded that most G-20 members will adopt mandatory clearing requirements or, as is the case with the United States and the EU, a combination of mandatory clearing requirements and economic incentives, to meet the G-20 commitment to have all standardized OTC derivatives contracts centrally cleared by year-end 2012.

Some countries, however, have expressed concern about "fair and open" access to central clearing parties.[56] In response, the Committee on Payment and Settlement Systems of the BIS produced a set of 24 principles for financial market infrastructures (FMIs), covering such areas as: general organization; credit and liquidity risk management; settlement; central securities depositories and exchange-of-value settlement systems; default management; general business and operational risk management; access; efficiency; and transparency. The Committee concluded that: "[F]air and open access to FMI (financial market infrastructures) services encourages competition among market participants and promotes efficient and low-cost clearing and settlement...participation requirements should therefore encourage broad access, including access by participants, other market infrastructures, and where relevant service providers in all relevant jurisdictions, based on reasonable risk-related participation requirements."[57]

Also, the FSB identified and is coordinating a set of four safeguards for a global framework to help authorities make informed decisions on the appropriate form of central counterparties (CCPs) to meet the G-20 commitment and to ensure that global CCPs do not introduce new systemic risks into the financial system. These four safeguards are:

1. Fair and open market access by market participants to CCPs, based on transparent and objective criteria;

2. Cooperative oversight arrangements between relevant authorities, both domestically and internationally and on either a bilateral or multilateral basis, that result in robust and consistently applied regulation and oversight of global CCPs;

3. Appropriate liquidity arrangements for CCPs in the currencies in which they clear; and

---

[55] *Jurisdictions' Declared Approaches to Central Clearing of OTC Derivatives*, Financial Stability Board, November 5, 2012.

[56] Silve, Joshua, Carolyn Wilkins, and Jonathan Witmer, Access to Central Clearing Services for Over-the-Counter Derivatives, *Financial System Review*, Bank of Canada, June 2011, p. 39-45.

[57] *Principles for Financial Market Infrastructures*, p. 101-102.

4. Robust resolution regimes to ensure that the core functions of CCPs are maintained during times of crisis and that consider the interests of all jurisdictions where the CCP is systemically important.[58]

As further guidance on these issues, the BIS published documents relating to the capital requirements for banks dealing with central counterparties[59] and on the recovery and resolution of such financial market infrastructures as CCPs.[60] The report on recovery and resolution provides guidance on the essential features of recovery and resolution regimes that are necessary "to ensure that the core function of the CCPs can be maintained during times of crisis and in a manner that considers the interests of all jurisdictions where the CCP is systemically important."[61]

Progress Developing International Standards for Exchange-Trading or Electronic Platform Trading

Issue. As previously indicated, the G-20 leaders agreed at the Pittsburgh Summit in September 2009 that all standardized OTC derivative contracts should be traded on exchanges or electronic trading platforms, where appropriate, and cleared through CCPs by the end of 2012. At the time of the summit, nearly 90% of derivatives contracts were transacted over-the-counter, or directly between two contracting parties without the use of an exchange or other intermediary.[62]

To assist in making the transition to trading platforms, the G-20 tasked the BIS and such other organizations as the International Organization of Securities Commissions (IOSCO) to provide guidance and recommendations. These organizations utilized a broad spectrum of legal and regulatory regimes that had been developed over time to regulate the trading of derivatives. In addition, there were existing, well-established international principles for securities regulation that include standards for the organization of secondary market trading. These legal and regulatory regimes and basic principles share a common purpose with the more current efforts at reform: ensuring that the trading architecture provides an orderly market that protects investors.

Whether measured by turnover, notional outstanding value, or number of contracts, approximately three-quarters of total derivatives are interest rate derivatives. Currently, trading platforms fall into two broad categories: those with multiple liquidity providers, or multi-dealer platforms;[63] and those with a single liquidity provider, or a single-dealer platform.[64] These

---

[58] *82nd Annual Report*, Bank for International Settlements, June 24, 2012, p. 82. Available at: http://www.bis.org/publ/arpdf/ar2012e.pdf.

[59] *Capital Requirements for Bank Exposures to Central Counterparties*, Bank for International Settlements, Basel Committee on Banking Supervision, July 2012. Available at: http://www.bis.org/publ/bcbs227.pdf.

[60] *Recovery and Resolution of Financial Market Infrastructures,* Bank for International Settlements, Committee on Payment and Settlement Systems, July 2012. Available at: http://www.bis.org/publ/cpss103.pdf.

[61] Ibid, p. 5.

[62] *Report on Trading of OTC Derivatives*, International Organization of Securities Commissions, February 2011, p. 4; and *Follow-on Analysis to the Report on trading of OTC Derivatives*, International Organization of Securities Commissions, January 2012.

[63] Multi-dealer trading platforms are defined as systems for the negotiation and execution of derivatives transactions where more than one dealer is ready to supply liquidity for derivatives transactions with counterparties that may seek such liquidity.

[64] A single-dealer trading platform provide for the bilateral negotiations of derivative contracts, or one in which one dealer is ready to supply liquidity for derivatives transactions with clients that may seek such liquidity.

platforms fulfill broadly the same function, but they may differ in the trade execution models they use to affect the transactions. There also may be differences in the participants that are covered by the various platforms: there may be differences in the degree of automation, the scope of asset class of products that are covered, and the geographic coverage. There are five common forms of trading platforms:

- An *order book system* which typically is fully automated and provides a system in which market participants can enter multiple bids and offers, observe bids and offers entered by other market participants, and choose to transact such bids and offers.

- A *market maker system* has one or more liquidity providers who are willing to deal on a regular or continuous basis against their proprietary capital by providing quotes to buy and sell financial instruments which are accessible to other participants in the system. Such systems can be organized on the basis of a single dealer, which acts as a counterparty to each trade, or on the basis of multiple dealers that compete for participant business.

- A *periodic auction system* in which orders are processed in batches at set intervals according to a pre-determined trading algorithm.

- A *bulletin board system* that provides an electronic quotation medium for market participants to originate, update, and display quotations in specific instruments.

- A *hybrid system* is a term that is used to describe a large variety of trading functionalities that have been refined to meet the needs of particular markets, and which may blend some of the functions of the other systems.

Progress. The FSB concluded in its October 2012 report that progress in enacting legislative and regulatory frameworks for implementing the commitment to trading standardized derivatives on exchanges and electronic platforms was markedly behind the progress made toward other commitments, that progress did not appear to be on track to meet the year-end 2012 deadline, and that the most important factor inhibiting the development of trading infrastructure was uncertainty over the regulatory framework.[65] As of October 2012, only the United States had adopted legislation that requires standardized derivatives be traded on exchanges and electronic platforms. Outside the United States, the derivatives classes for which organized platform trading are most widely available are credit default swaps and interest rate swaps. The FSB argues that, at the very least, requiring transparency in reporting the price and volume of OTC derivatives transactions should serve to inform decisions regarding mandatory organized platform trading.[66]

Latest Developments. According to the FSB's October 2012 survey, the most commonly cited reason for the lack of more widespread development and use of organized trading platforms is uncertainty about the scope and form of requirements for OTC derivatives to be traded on organized trading platforms.[67] In addition, market infrastructure operators face challenges in creating the appropriate technology to interface with clients and other infrastructure, which could create efficiencies that would create incentives to build links with other infrastructure. The FSB also concluded that:

---

[65] *OTC Derivatives Market Reforms: Fourth Progress Report, p. 36.*

[66] *OTC Derivatives Market Reforms: Third Progress Report*, p. 4.

[67] *OTC Derivatives Market Reforms: Fourth Progress Report*, p. 38.

1. Trading infrastructure is less developed than infrastructure for central clearing and trade reporting, due to uncertainties about the scope and form of future regulatory frameworks for organized platform trading.

2. Organized trading platforms currently are available for trading certain derivatives products, primarily credit and interest rate swaps.

3. Features of existing organized trading platforms vary, reflecting a range of characteristics.

4. Most of the organized trading platforms are headquartered in Europe or the United States, with global online access and local offices and trading screens in other markets.

5. The extent that organized trading platforms are linked to other infrastructure varies, but is likely to increase.

6. New trading platforms are expected to become operational relatively quickly once regulatory frameworks for mandatory organized platform trading are put in place.

7. Some degree of product standardization is a prerequisite for an OTC derivative to be transacted on an organized trading platform. Steps to increase product standardization can lead to improved market liquidity, pricing, and transparency.[68]

Progress in Reporting OTC Derivatives Trades to Trade Repositories (TR)

Issue. Trade repositories are intended to provide national authorities with a global view of the OTC derivatives markets through full and timely access to the data they need to carry out their respective mandates. This mandate includes: a) assessing systemic risk and financial stability; b) conducting market surveillance and enforcement; c) supervising market participants; and d) conducting resolution activities. In the FSB's October 2012 survey, it concluded that TRs (except for two TRs located in the European Union) predominantly serve market participants located in their home jurisdictions.[69]

Progress. The FSB has concluded that currently there is no single, industry-wide format for data reporting, processing and storage of OTC derivatives trade data. This lack of a common format compromises one of the major objectives of the reporting requirement: the ability to aggregate OTC derivatives data across multiple TRs to support the objectives of supervisory and regulatory authorities. This issue is being addressed in a number of ways, including the development of a global Legal Entity Identifier (LEI) system through the FSB, which noted that the finance sector lags behind other industries in agreeing on and introducing a consistent global framework for entity identification.[70] The LEI system is considered to be an important "building block" in contributing to and facilitating such financial stability objectives as: 1) improved risk

---

[68] *Ibid*, p. 36.

[69] *Ibid.* p. 28.

[70] *A Global Legal Entity Identifier for Financial Markets*, Financial Stability Board, June 8, 2012, p. 1. Available at: http://www.financialstabilityboard.org/publications/r_120608.pdf.

management in firms; 2) better assessment of micro and macroprudential risks; 3) facilitation of orderly resolution; 4) containing market abuse and curbing financial fraud; and 5) enabling higher quality and accuracy of financial data overall.[71] As a first step, the FSB proposed the development of a Regulatory Oversight Committee (ROC) charged with responsibility for the governance of the global LEI system. A draft charter for the ROC was approved by the G-20 members in November 2012, and the ROC became operational in January, 2013. Currently, the ROC is comprised of 45 authorities, primarily central banks, and 15 observers. The United States is represented by the Board of Governors of the Federal Reserve System, the Department of the Treasury, the Commodity Futures Trading Commission, the Office of the Comptroller of the Currency, the Federal Deposit Insurance Corporation, and the Securities and Exchange Commission. The Federal Reserve Bank of New York has observer status.[72]

Latest Developments. The FSB October 2012 report also concluded that:

1. TRs exist for reporting in each of the five asset classes (foreign exchange contracts; interest rate contracts; equity-linked contracts; commodity contracts; and credit default swaps), with the greatest progress being made in reporting credit, interest rate, and equity derivatives.

2. A number of TRs are planning to extend the asset classes for which they accept trade reporting.

3. Few TRs currently have links to other FMIs.

4. The majority of TRs report that the G-15 dealers are either ready now to comply with mandatory trade reporting or are expected to be ready by year-end 2012.

5. TRs' estimates of the time required for new clients to complete the necessary administrative and technological steps to register with a TR and start trade reporting vary from six weeks to three months.

6. There is considerable commonality in the categories of data that are collected and stored by TRs, but there is no single standard format for data reporting and storage and the majority of TRs use proprietary codes and formats, which makes aggregation and reconciliation difficult.

7. Less than half of the TRs surveyed collect data or provide services in relation to portfolio-level information.

8. All TRs report maintaining a range of data security arrangements and safeguards.

9. All TRs provide access for authorities to data stored and to the public in an anonymous and aggregated form.[73]

---

[71] *Ibid*, p. 1.

[72] *Implementing the Global Legal Entity Identifier (LEI) System – A Charter for the Regulatory Oversight Committee and Report on Progress*: Note for the G-20 Finance ministers and Central Bank Governors Meeting November 4/5, 2012, Financial Stability Board, October 31, 2012; *Fifth Progress Note on the Global LEI Initiative*, Financial Stability Board, January 11, 2012; and *The Regulatory Oversight Committee for the Global Legal Entity Identifier (LEI) System*, Financial Stability board, January 11, 2012.

[73] *OTC Derivatives Market Reforms: Fourth Progress Report*, p. 26.

Progress Implementing International Standards for Capital Requirements

Issue. The Basel Committee on Banking Supervision (BCBS) supported a number of reforms of international standards to ensure that banks have appropriate risk coverage of counterparty credit risk exposures arising from OTC derivatives transactions as part of the Basel III capital framework. The Basel III reforms concerning OTC derivatives strengthen the capital requirements for counterparty credit risk (CCR), or the risk that the counterparty to a transaction is unable or unwilling to meet its obligations. For non-centrally cleared OTC derivatives, banks will be subject to a credit valuation adjustment charge, or the adjustment that quantifies the potential loss caused by changes in the credit quality of the counterparty.

Progress. In July 2012, the BCBS issued interim rules on capital requirements for bank exposures to central clearing parties and to clients for whom they perform central clearing services. The capital requirements are meant to ensure that the core functions of central clearing parties, and other types of financial market infrastructures, can be maintained during a crisis, especially when the CCP is considered to be systemically important.[74]

In large part, these rules are intended to create incentives for market participants to use CCPs. The interim rules set a nominal risk weight for banks that act as a clearing member of a CCP for their own purposes or on behalf of clients of 2% for trade exposures to a CCP that is supervised, among other requirements.[75] Despite opposition from banks, they will be required to hold capital against the prospect that they may be compelled by market events to draw upon their default fund, something they have not had to do to date. The interim rules also require that banks apply a default risk of 1250% to their default fund contributions of a non-qualifying CCP.[76]

When the BIS proposed placing capital requirements on banks for exposure to centrally cleared derivatives, it also addressed the issue of risk exposure to non-centrally cleared derivatives by proposing margin requirements. In particular, the BIS argued that such margin requirements on non-centrally cleared derivatives are necessary in order to: 1) mitigate systemic risk associated with the large volumes of OTC derivatives that are not sufficiently standardized for central clearing; 2) ensure that collateral is available to offset losses caused by the default of a counterparty; and 3) limit the buildup of uncollateralized exposures in the financial system.[77] The BIS argued further that margin requirements that reflect the higher risk associated with non-centrally cleared derivatives "complement and support" the G-20 derivatives market reforms, because they promote central clearing by addressing "financial incentives that might otherwise induce market participants to customize contracts and thereby avoid the costs of clearing that arise from CCP's requirements for margin."[78]

Latest Developments. The European Banking Authority (EBA) published its final draft regulations on capital requirements for central counterparties on September 26, 2012. According to these standards the capital of a European CCP should at least be equal to the sum of: 1) the

---

[74] *Recovery and Resolution of Financial Market Infrastructures*, p. 1.

[75] *Capital Requirements for Bank Exposures to Central Counterparties*, p. 3.

[76] *Ibid*, p. 12.

[77] *OTC Derivatives Market Reforms: Fourth Progress Report*, p. 40.

[78] *Ibid*, p. 40.

CCP's gross operational expenses during the time needed to wind down or restructure its activities; 2) the capital necessary to cover the overall operational and legal risks; 3) the capital necessary to cover credit, counterparty credit and market risks not covered by specific financial resources; and 4) business risk, to be determined by each CCP and the approval of the relevant authority.[79]

Overall Assessment of Progress

The FSB is charged with monitoring and reporting on the progress the G-20 nations have made in changing laws and regulations implementing the G-20 recommendations. The latest FSB progress report on OTC derivatives market reforms was published in October 2012, with another report expected to be published in April 2013. **Table 2** provides a summary of the progress G-20 members and some FSB members have made in adopting and implementing legislation and regulations regarding OTC derivatives markets. Some countries, principally those with limited derivatives markets, tend to lag behind other countries, such as the United States, with advanced and extensive derivatives markets. According to the FSB data in **Table 2**, the surveyed countries have made the most progress in adopting measures regarding reporting to trade repositories and the least progress in implementing margin requirements for non-centrally traded derivatives. The report is based on a questionnaire sent to the FSB member countries covering the members' work plans and progress to date in implementing OTC derivatives market reforms. Although the survey generally solicits simple Yes/No responses, the survey also requests detailed explanations on some issues. Responses by the individual FSB members are available to the members, but are not provided to the public. For individual country detail, see **Appendix B** to this report.

The FSB concluded in its October 2012 report that Australia, the European Union, Hong Kong, Japan, and the United States had progressed in implementing regulations governing central clearing and reporting to trade repositories.[80] The FSB concluded that the countries surveyed are committed to changing their legislative and regulatory framework to achieve the G-20 objectives, but that some jurisdictions were "waiting for key elements of the regulatory framework in the EU, Japan, and the United States to be finalized before putting their own legislation in place."[81] The FSB also noted that important standard setting bodies had made "significant" progress in developing the international policies that facilitate the advancement of OTC derivatives reform across jurisdictions and that those jurisdictions needed to "promptly develop and implement legislative and regulatory frameworks." The FSB concluded, however:

> But legislation and regulation are not by themselves enough. Market participants need to take practical steps to ensure that the necessary market infrastructure is available by further expanding the number and scope of OTC derivatives transactions that are standardized, centrally cleared, traded on organized platforms and reported to TRs. Failure to implement the commitments by the agreed deadline risks a loss of momentum for reform, in addition to failing to deliver the benefits of improved transparency, mitigation of systemic risk, and protection against market abuse.[82]

---

[79] *EBA Final Draft Regulatory Technical Standards on Capital Requirements for Central Counterparties Under Regulation (EU) No. 648/2012*, European Banking Authority, September 26, 2012, p. 3.

[80] *OTC Derivatives Market Reforms: Fourth Progress Report*, p. 42.

[81] *OTC Derivatives Market Reforms: Third Progress Report*, p. 1.

[82] *Ibid*, p. 2.

Table 3. Summary Progress of OTC Derivatives Market Reforms

Status of applicable legislation

	Central clearing	Exchanges/ Platform trading	Reporting to Trade Repositories	Capital Reserves	Margin Require-ments	Standardization
Argentina	Adopted	Adopted	NA	NA	NA	NA
Australia	Proposed	Proposed	Proposed	Proposed	NA	Proposed
Brazil	NA	NA	Adopted	Adopted	NA	NA
Canada	Proposed	Adopted	Adopted	NA	NA	NA
China	Proposed	Adopted	Adopted	NA	NA	Adopted
European Union	Adopted	Proposed	Adopted	NA	NA	Adopted
Hong Kong	Proposed	Proposed	Proposed	Adopted	Proposed	Proposed
India	Adopted	Adopted	Adopted	Adopted	Adopted	Adopted
Indonesia	NA	Adopted	Adopted	NA	NA	Adopted
Japan	Adopted	Adopted	Adopted	NA	NA	Adopted
Mexico	NA	NA	NA	NA	NA	NA
Korea	Proposed	NA	Adopted	NA	NA	Proposed
Russia	Adopted	Adopted	Adopted	NA	NA	Adopted
Saudi Arabia	NA	NA	NA	NA	NA	NA
Singapore	Proposed	Proposed	Proposed	Proposed	NA	Consultation
South Africa	Proposed	NA	Proposed	NA	NA	Proposed
Switzerland	Consultation	Consultation	Partially Adopted	Adopted	NA	Consultation
Turkey	Proposed	NA	Proposed	NA	NA	NA
United States	Adopted	Adopted	Adopted	Adopted	Adopted	Adopted

Source: OTC Derivatives Market Reforms: Fourth Progress Report on Implementation, Financial Stability Board, October 31, 2012, p. 13.

In October 2012, the FSB offered three general conclusions concerning the state of regulatory development of OTC derivatives trading among the G-20 members:

1. Market infrastructures regarding OTC derivatives trading, central clearing, and reporting are in place and can be scaled up;

2. The international policy work on the four safeguards (fair and open markets, cooperative oversight arrangements, liquidity arrangements, and robust resolution regimes) for clearing derivatives through global counterparties is substantially completed and implementation is proceeding at a national level; and

3. The most significant impediment to further progress appears to be uncertainty regarding the regulatory framework.[83]

In addition to the general conclusions, the FSB issued a series of specific conclusions regarding the readiness of the G-20 members to meet the self-imposed deadline of year-end 2012 for implementing major reforms in the OTC derivatives market. According to the FSB:

1. Market infrastructure has been set up to provide services to a wide range of the global OTC derivatives markets, including clearing counterparties, that are capable of clearing some products in all asset classes and trade repositories exist for reporting transactions in all asset classes.

2. The proportion of transactions reported to TRs and centrally cleared has plateaued due to uncertainty over the future regulatory framework.

3. Further clarity and consensus regarding "standardization" is needed in order to reduce the risk of regulatory arbitrage in the application of central clearing and organized platform trading requirements.

4. The financial sector should accelerate its work on standardization of both products and processes to increase the use of standardization.

5. Adding new products and participants to organized trading platforms and to trade repositories takes from between six months to more than a year.

6. Trade repositories have become an important source of data for authorities; however, significant gaps remain concerning the extent of reporting and the central clearing of products.

7. Impediments to aggregating data may limit progress in further developing the use of trade repositories for regulatory and financial stability purposes.

8. The FSB supports ongoing efforts to improve authorities' access to TR data and guidance on access to TR data.

Other International Policy Developments

On November 28, 2012, financial market regulators from Australia, Brazil, the European Union, Hong Kong, Japan, Canada, Singapore, Switzerland, and the United States met to discuss progress to date in reforming the OTC derivatives markets and to address cross-border regulatory issues. In a statement, the regulators indicated they support robust and consistent standards in and across jurisdictions, but that complete harmonization, or the perfect alignment of rules across jurisdictions, is unlikely given different legal systems and market conditions.[84] They also indicated that their objective is to prevent regulatory gaps, reduce the potential for arbitrage opportunities, and foster a level playing field for market participants, intermediaries, and infrastructures. They also indicated that conflicting, inconsistent, or duplicative rules inhibit the execution or clearing of cross-border transactions or impose additional compliance burdens.

---

[83] *OTC Derivatives Market Reforms, Fourth Progress Report*, p. 1.

[84] Joint Press Statement of the Leaders on Operating Principles and Areas of exploration in the Regulation of the Cross-Border OTC Derivatives Market, November 28, 2012. Available at: http://www.sec.gov/news/press/2012/2012-251.htm.

As a result of these concerns, the regulators reached mutual understanding in four areas of principles and areas for exploration. These are listed below.

1. **Understanding on Clearing Determinants.** The regulators agreed to consult prior to making a final determination regarding which derivatives products will be subject to mandatory clearing requirements. In addition, they agreed that once one of the authorities has decided that a certain product or class of products should be subject to a clearing requirement, then each of the other authorities will consider whether to follow suit.

2. **Understanding on Sharing of Information and Supervisory and Enforcement Cooperation**. The regulators agreed to adopt supervisory cooperation arrangements to enable effective supervision and oversight of cross-border activity and a bilateral enforcement agreement to provide other national authorities with assistance.

3. **Understanding on Timing.** While attempting to meet the G-20 timetable of implementing clearing, reporting, trading, and capital requirements by year-end 2012, the regulators acknowledged that differences in implementation dates may create gaps in regulations and uncertainty in the application of certain cross-border regulatory requirements and may lead to risks to financial markets. As a result, the regulators agreed to a "reasonable, limited" transition period to facilitate the implementation of cross-border regulations in appropriate circumstances and in consultation with other jurisdictions.

4. **Areas of Exploration.** The regulators agreed to follow one of a number of approaches to regulating cross-border activities when more than one set of rules applies: a) recognize the rules or oversight of another authority; b) as part of a registration requirement, allow foreign regulations to substitute for applicable domestic regulations; c) allow foreign regulations to substitute for compliance with otherwise applicable transaction-level requirements; d) provide different sets of registration categories or provide for the same regulatory requirements to be observed in different ways based on characteristics and activities.

Progress in Major Foreign OTC Derivatives Markets

European Union

On July 4, 2012, the European Parliament[85] and the European Council approved the European Market Infrastructure Regulation (EMIR), which entered into force on August 16, 2012, as the main legislative device for reforming the OTC derivatives market in the EU.[86] The regulation[87] has five major objectives: 1) establish clearing obligations for certain classes of OTC derivatives;

---

[85] For additional information about the European Parliament see: CRS Report RS21998, *The European Parliament*, by Kristin Archick.

[86] Regulation No. 648/2012 of the European Parliament and of the Council July 4, 2012 on OTC Derivatives, Central Counterparties, and Trade Repositories, *Official Journal of the European Union*, July 27, 2012.

[87] Regulations become laws in each member state without further implementing legislation; Directives generally require each member state to pass legislation and the states can use their own discretion in deciding how to implement the Directive.

2) establish risk mitigation techniques for non-centrally cleared OTC derivatives; 3) establish reporting obligations to trade repositories; 4) establish organizational, conduct of business, and prudential requirements for central clearing parties; and 5) establish requirements for trade repositories, including the duty to make certain data available to the public and to relevant authorities. The EMIR requires the central clearing of all standardized OTC derivatives contracts that are judged to be subject to the clearing obligation. The definition of a standardized OTC derivatives contract follows the one developed by the FSB.[88] The European Securities and Markets Authority (ESMA) developed draft technical standards after soliciting public comments. The standards specify the criteria for identifying those OTC derivatives that will be covered by the central clearing obligation, prudential requirements for CCPs, and the data to be reported to trade repositories.

The European Commission expected to approve the standards by the end of 2012 and implement them in the first quarter of 2013. On February 6, 2013, however, the Economic and Monetary Affairs Committee (ECON) of the European Parliament voted to reject two of the six proposed regulations proposed by the ESMA.[89] The two regulations concerned: 1) indirect clearing arrangements, the clearing obligation, the public register, access to a trading venue, non-financial counterparties, risk mitigation techniques for OTC derivatives contracts not cleared by a central counterparty; and 2) requirements for central counterparties. ECON's rejection of the proposed rules was sent to the European Parliament on February 6, 2013 for consideration. Parliament's approval of ECON's recommendation was expected to delay implementation of any of the proposed rules for at least six months. Faced with such a prospect, the European Parliament and the ESMA reached a compromise deal on February 7, 2013 that allowed energy and technology companies among non-financial firms, which deemed the standards to be too burdensome, to postpone implementation of the proposed standards for three years. The remaining standards will be implemented around mid-March 2013.[90]

The European Union has addressed the issue of the cross-border application of rules and regulations on OTC derivatives markets through the EMIR and proposed revisions of the Markets in Financial Instruments Directive and Regulation (MiFID and MiFIR). The EMIR contains a mechanism that attempts to avoid duplicative or conflicting rules, including a process for recognizing "equivalent" regimes in other jurisdictions where specified conditions are met.[91] The EMIR permits the EC to declare that the legal, supervisory, and enforcement arrangements of another jurisdiction are equivalent to those in the EMIR for clearing and reporting obligations, risk mitigation techniques, non-financial counterparties, and implementing the framework. Where such a decision exists, an EU counterparty transacting with a foreign counterparty can apply the foreign jurisdiction's rules and be judged to have complied with its obligations under the EMIR.

The EMIR also provides for recognition of foreign CCPs and foreign TRs, which allow a CCP or TR established outside the EU to provide its services to EU entities. To qualify, the EC must

---

[88] The FSB definition of a standardized contract involves three factors: degree of standardization of a product's contractual terms and operational processes; the depth and liquidity of the market for the product in question; and the availability of fair, reliable and generally accepted pricing sources.

[89] *Statement by Commissioner Michel Barnier on the Technical Standards to Implement the New Rules on Derivatives*, February 7, 2013. Available at: http://ec.europa.eu/commission_2010-2014/barnier/docs/speeches/20130207_emir_en.pdf

[90] Brunsden, Jim, Non-Financial Firms to Get 3-Year Delay on Swaps Ruled, EU Says, *Bloomberg*, February 7, 2013.

[91] Regulation 648/2012, par 58.

---

determine that the foreign entity is subject to equivalent rules and supervision and the European Securities and Markets Authority (ESMA) must have a cooperation agreement with the foreign authorities. Similarly, foreign trade repositories must be judged by the EC to be subject to equivalent rules and standards of supervision in its country of origin, there must be an international agreement between the EU and each foreign authority, and cooperation agreements with ESMA and the foreign authorities.

Hong Kong

The Hong Kong Monetary Authority (HKMA) and the Securities and Futures Commission of Hong Kong (SFC) have developed proposals to implement all of the OTC derivatives market reforms recommended by the G-20 countries.[92] Hong Kong also began consultations on the scope of certain newly-introduced regulated activities and the regulation of systemically important entities, which the Hong Kong authorities intend to have incorporated into proposed legislation by early 2013. Although the proposals indicate that no requirement will be mandated to require derivatives be traded on organized trading platforms, such an option is available to the regulators and potentially could be implemented following the completion of additional research into the best process to implement such a requirement. Currently, the proposed framework for regulating OTC derivatives includes defining the scope of the term "OTC derivatives transactions;" products subject to mandatory reporting and clearing; application of mandatory reporting obligations; application of mandatory clearing obligations; regulation of CCPs; capital and margin requirements; regulation of intermediaries; and oversight of "systemically important players."

The Hong Kong proposal also will allow CCPs to accept members from other entities regulated by an "acceptable overseas jurisdiction" as determined by the HKMA and SFC. In addition, Hong Kong has added location requirements for reporting to trade repositories. All derivatives transactions that have a bearing on Hong Kong's financial markets would be required to be reported to the HKMA trade repository, reportedly to allow the Hong Kong authorities to obtain relevant OTC derivatives information as quickly and directly as possible.[93] Hong Kong provides for exceptions for both clearing and reporting for central banks, monetary or similar bodies and certain global institutions, and clearing exemptions for intra-group transactions, transactions involving non-financial entity end-users engaged in commercial hedging activities, and transactions involving "closed market" participants.[94]

Japan

On September 6, 2012, the Japanese Diet approved revised legislation on the use of electronic trading platforms and market transparency. This legislation will be phased in over three years to give market participants time to comply fully with the new requirements. Initially, the requirements will apply to OTC derivatives, primarily Japanese yen-denominated interest rate

---

[92] *Joint Consultations Conclusions on the Proposed Regulatory Regime for the Over-the-Counter Derivatives Market in Hong Kong*, Hong Kong Monetary Authority, July, 2012. Available at: http://www.hkma.gov.hk/media/eng/doc/key-information/press-release/2012/20120711e3a34.pdf.

[93] *OTC Derivatives Market Reforms, Fourth Progress Report*, p. 45.

[94] Closed market participants are described as jurisdictions which have a material level of foreign exchange control or other local regulatory restrictions making it impractical to require that clearing take place in any jurisdiction other than its own.

---

swaps, which are standardized and maintain adequate liquidity. The plan envisages that yen-denominated interest rate swaps will be subject to mandatory clearing requirements, with the scope of products expanded to include foreign currency (both US dollar and euro) denominated interest rate swaps and credit default swaps referenced to Japanese companies. In addition, mandatory clearing requirements will be applied to transactions in OTC derivatives products that are subject to mandatory clearing between large domestic financial institutions registered under the Financial Instruments Exchange Act (FIEA), that are members of the clearing organization the Japan Securities Clearing Corporation (JSCC), or that are subsidiaries of a parent company that is a member of JSCC. This requirement could be expanded to include foreign financial institutions under certain conditions.

According to the new legislation, financial institutions registered the FIEA will be required to report their OTC derivatives transactions to trade repositories. Such TRs will be available for credit derivatives transactions and forward, option, and swap transactions.

A detailed look at the FSB's assessments of each G-20 country's progress in implementing reforms, based on each country's responses to a survey provided by the FSB semi-annually, is provided in the Appendix to this report.

Issues for Congress

Congress has addressed directly the governance of the derivatives market through the Dodd-Frank Wall Street Reform and Consumer Protection Act (P.L. 111-203). The Dodd-Frank Act, in its Title VII on OTC derivatives reform, addresses each of the major G-20 commitments. Often, final implementation is left to the relevant executive agencies, particularly the CFTC and the SEC – though with additional roles for the prudential regulators. Section 722 of the Dodd-Frank Act amended the Commodity Exchange Act's section 2 to limit the applicability of the Act's swaps market reforms so that they "shall not apply to activities outside the United States unless those activities—"(1) have a direct and significant connection with activities in, or effect on, commerce of the United States."[1] However, the Act left to the CFTC to determine which such activities related to the swaps markets do have such a direct and significant connection. Congress would have an oversight role in this CFTC determination – an important one, due to the global nature of the OTC derivatives markets.

On July 12, 2012, the CFTC issued proposed guidance on "Cross-Border Application of Certain Swaps Provisions of the Commodity Exchange Act."[2] The guidance was aimed at setting out how certain requirements in Title VII, such as the clearing, trade execution, registration of a person as a swap dealer or major swap participant, and other reporting and recordkeeping provisions, would apply to cross-border swaps that may be transacted across national boundaries. Under the guidance, foreign firms that do more than a de minimus amount of OTC derivatives markets activity as swap dealers would register with the CFTC.[95] Foreign firms that do register

---

[1] P.L. 111-203, Section 722.

[2] Commodity Futures Trading Commission, "Cross-Border Application of Certain Swaps Provisions of the Commodity Exchange Act," 77, No. 134 *Federal Register* 41214, July 12, 2012. Available at: http://www.cftc.gov/ucm/groups/public/@lrfederalregister/documents/file/2012-16496a.pdf.

[95] Testimony of Gary Gensler, Chairman, Commodity Futures Trading Commission Before the U.S. House Financial Services Subcommittee on Capital Markets and Government-Sponsored Enterprises, December 12, 2012, p. 7.

with the CFTC, however, would be allowed to substitute compliance with a comparable and comprehensive foreign regulatory regime, for U.S. regulatory compliance.[96] This potential for substituted foreign compliance further invokes a determination of how much regulatory progress other G-20 countries have achieved in derivatives reforms, in comparison to the United States. Again, Congress is involved through its oversight of the CFTC, which will make these assessments.

This determination by the agency could potentially affect U.S. businesses with foreign operations and their dealings with non-U.S. clients and foreign businesses with U.S. operations. Indeed, the 112th Congress considered legislation seeking to address questions raised by the extraterritorial nature of the global swaps market and the Dodd-Frank provisions. Bills introduced in the 112th Congress included H.R. 2779, exempting from the clearing requirement most swaps between corporate affiliates in the United States and abroad. H.R. 2779 passed the House in the 112th Congress. Also, H.R. 3283 expressly limited the extraterritorial reach of Dodd-Frank by exempting swaps and security based swaps between U.S. and non-U.S. persons (except for reporting requirements).

Such agency rulemakings and proposed legislation raise broad questions for congressional oversight or potential new legislation, such as the following:

- What connections to the United States would require a non-U.S. person to register as a swap dealer or major swap participant?

- Which Dodd-Frank Act requirements should apply to the OTC derivatives, or swaps, activities of non-U.S. persons?

- What about to U.S. persons, and their branches, subsidiaries and affiliates outside of the United States?

- To the extent that Title VII of the Dodd-Frank requirements would apply, under what circumstances should U.S. authorities permit non-U.S. person to comply with the regulatory regime of a foreign jurisdiction instead of complying with U.S. requirements?

A look at progress achieved by foreign regimes in implementing these G-20 commitments should help members of Congress and U.S regulators in deliberating these questions.

Conclusions

Following the financial crisis of 2008-2009, national leaders in the G-20 have spearheaded reforms in the rules and regulations governing the trading of financial instruments known as derivatives. While these reforms are being implemented, Congress may choose to monitor them carefully to assess the comparability between regulations adopted in the United States and those adopted abroad in markets that serve as competitors for U.S. financial services firms. The objective of these reforms is to establish criteria for standardizing derivatives contracts and to have those contracts traded on organized trading markets through central counterparties that have a capital base that is sufficient to cover any risk exposure. In addition, the data on standardized contracts is expected to be reported to trade repositories and made available to regulators and

---

[96] Ibid.

policymakers in order to assess the stability and performance of the derivatives market. These reforms are being addressed through regulatory changes in five areas: 1) standardizing OTC derivatives contracts; 2) developing international standards and policy for central clearing and for risk management of non-centrally cleared derivatives; 3) developing international standards and policy for exchanges or electronic platform trading; 4) developing the infrastructure to facilitate reporting OTC transactions to trade repositories (TR); and 5) developing and implementing international standards and policies for capital requirements.

In addition, as regulators in the United States, the European Union and elsewhere craft new rules to govern the OTC derivatives markets, they confront the challenge of regulating domestic activity in markets that are fundamentally international in scope. While market participants generally have accepted the fact that the OTC derivatives markets will be reformed, they are closely monitoring how those reforms are implemented and instances of differences in implementation or regulatory arbitrage. As implementation proceeds in both the United States and abroad, Congress may be pressed at times to amend current measures.

The FSB has been tasked by the G-20 to coordinate and report on the progress its members have made in adopting various derivatives market reforms. According to the latest report, the surveyed countries are making progress in such areas as having derivatives contracts centrally cleared and reported to trade repositories, but lag behind in standardizing contracts, building up capital reserves, and having contracts traded through exchanges or on electronic platforms. Without a generally accepted definition of what constitutes a standardized derivatives contract, data reported to trade repositories will not be comparable, which would greatly reduce the ability of regulators to make assessments of the state of the derivatives markets. Another key issue is the comparability of reforms across the surveyed countries. While countries are ostensibly meeting the reform objectives of the G-20, it is not possible to assess the quality of the current reforms and the potential for regulatory arbitrage. This is particularly true for G-20 members that currently are not hosts to large volumes of derivatives trading and may have relatively under-developed capital markets.

As a result of a survey of the efforts made to date by G-20 members and some FSB members, the Financial Stability Board concluded in October 2012 that:

- Regulators and derivatives market participants were struggling to meet their commitments to implement market reforms by the end of 2012. While significant progress has been made in constructing the architecture for standardizing, clearing, and reporting derivatives contracts, regulators are juggling sometimes conflicting objectives. In particular, market participants are pressuring regulators to develop a common set of rules to reduce the prospects of regulatory arbitrage and to reduce regulatory uncertainties in cross-border transactions.

- Regulators in a number of countries surveyed by the FSB are closely gauging their own actions to ensure that any regulations they propose are aligned with those of the market leaders, principally the United States and the European Union. In addition, few of the surveyed countries have adopted measures for building capital reserves.

- Various countries face impediments in reforming the way derivatives are traded and reported, the most important being uncertainty over the regulatory framework that is being developed in the United States and European Union.

- As a group, the G-20 countries and the FSB members have committed to adopting legislation and regulations to fully implement the G-20 reforms, but few nations have progressed as far as the United States and most are either drafting or still finalizing regulations. According to the FSB, the market infrastructure is mostly in place for greater coordination of efforts regarding standardizing, clearing, and reporting on derivatives contracts. A lack of regulatory conformity, however, appears to be impeding progress. For instance, market leaders remain uncertain over the definition of what constitutes a standardized derivatives contract and, therefore, are hesitant to adopt regulations on clearing and reporting relative to standardized derivatives contracts.

- Trade repositories are positioned to report on each of the five asset classes (foreign exchange contracts; interest rate contracts; equity-linked contracts; commodity contracts; and credit default swaps). Nevertheless, there is no single standard format for data reporting and storage and the majority of TRs use proprietary codes and formats, which make aggregation and reconciliation difficult, thereby undermining one of the main objectives in collecting and reporting data on derivatives contracts. Furthermore, these efforts are closely tied to efforts to overcome the lack of a single, industry-wide format for data reporting, processing and storage of OTC derivatives trade data. This lack of a common format defeats one of the major objectives of the reporting requirement: the ability to aggregate OTC derivatives data across multiple TRs to support the objectives of supervisory and regulatory authorities.

Appendix A. Glossary

Bank for International Settlements (BIS): headquartered in Basel, Switzerland, BIS serves the specialized needs of central banks and international organizations by promoting collaboration among central banks, conducting research, acting as a prime counterparty for central banks in their financial transactions, and serving as an agent or trustee in connection with international financial operations.

Basel Committee on Banking Supervision (BCBS): provides a forum for cooperation on banking supervisory matters by working to improve the quality of banking supervision worldwide; it seeks to reach a common understanding of key supervisory issues by exchanging information on national supervisory issues, approaches and techniques; at times, the BCBS uses this common understanding to develop guidelines and supervisory standards, in particular in the area of international standards on capital adequacy, the Core Principles for Effective Banking Supervision and the Concordat on cross-border banking supervision.

Central Counterparties (CCPs): act as intermediaries between counterparties to contracts traded in one or more financial markets in a central counterparty system; acts as the buyer to every seller and the seller to every buyer, through a system known as novation (an open-offer system of legally binding contracts), thereby ensuring the performance of open contracts; generally attempts to reduce risks to participants by requiring participants to provide collateral to cover current and potential future exposures.

Collateralized Debt Obligations (CDOs): are a type of structured asset-backed security whose value and payments are derived from a portfolio of fixed-income underlying assets; CDOs are assigned different risk classes or tranches, with "senior" tranches considered to be the safest. Since interest and principal payments are made in order of seniority, junior tranches offer higher coupon payments (and interest rates) or lower prices to compensate for additional default risk. Investors, pension funds, and insurance companies buy CDOs. CDOs based on sub-prime mortgages were at the heart of the 2008-2009 global financial crises.

Committee on Payment and Settlement Systems (CPSS): established in 1990 by the G-10 countries to address general concerns regarding the efficiency and stability of payment, clearing, settlement, and related arrangements; focuses on issues related to these systems or arrangements and to their relations with the major financial markets for the conduct of monetary policy; and undertakes specific studies at the request of the Governors or on its own initiative. The CPSS is comprised of the central bank Governors of 25 central banks.

Credit Default Swaps (CDS): are a credit derivative contract between two counterparties in which the buyer makes periodic payments to the seller and in return receives a sum of money if a certain credit event occurs (such as a default in an underlying financial instrument). Payoffs and collateral calls on CDSs issued on sub-prime mortgage CDOs were a primary cause of the problems of American International Group, Inc. (AIG) and other companies in the financial crisis.

European Market Infrastructure Regulation (EMIR): is legislation that was adopted by the European Commission in July 2012 and became effective in August 2012 to implement reforms in the over-the-counter derivatives market. Reforms include: reporting obligations for OTC derivatives; clearing obligations for eligible OTC derivatives; measures to reduce counterparty credit risk and operational risk for bilaterally-cleared OTC derivatives; common rules for central counterparties (CCPs) and for trade repositories; and rules on the establishment of interoperability between CCPs.

European Securities and Market Authority (ESMA): an independent EU authority that helps safeguard the stability of the EU's financial system by ensuring the integrity, transparency, efficiency and orderly functioning of securities markets, and by enhancing investor protection. The ESMA attempts to improve supervisory convergence among securities regulators and across financial sectors by working closely with the other European Supervisory Authorities competent in the field of banking (EBA), and insurance and occupational pensions (EIOPA). (See http://www.bis.org/publ/cpss101a.pdf.)

European Banking Authority (EBA): established by the European Parliament and Council in November 2010; it assumed the existing and ongoing tasks and responsibilities from the Committee of European Banking Supervisors (CEBS). The EBA acts as the hub in a network of EU and national bodies safeguarding the stability of the financial system, the transparency of markets and financial products, and the protection of depositors and investors. It also acts to prevent regulatory arbitrage, guarantee a level playing field, strengthen international supervisory coordination, promote supervisory convergence, and provide advice to the EU institutions in the areas of banking, payments and e-money regulation and issues related to corporate governance, auditing and financial reporting. (See http://www.eba.europa.eu/.)

Financial Market Infrastructures (FMIs): are generally viewed as systemically important multilateral payment systems among participating institutions that facilitate the clearing, settlement, and recording of monetary and other financial transactions, such as payments, securities, and derivatives contracts. According to the BIS, FMIs provide participants with centralized clearing, settlement, and recording of financial transactions among themselves or between each of them and a central party to allow for greater efficiency and reduced costs and risks. Some FMIs are critical in helping central banks conduct monetary policy and maintain financial stability. (see *Principles for Financial Market Infrastructures*, Bank for International Settlements, April 2012 (http://www.bis.org/publ/cpss101a.pdf.).

Financial Stability Board (FSB): was created at the G-20 London Summit in April 2009 as the successor to the Financial Stability Forum; its mission is to coordinate and monitor at the international level the work of national financial authorities and international standard-setting bodies, in the interest of financial stability. The FSB is chaired by Mark Carney, Governor of the Bank of Canada; its Secretariat is hosted by the BIS. U.S. members consist of the Department of the Treasury, the Board of Governors of the Federal Reserve System, and the Securities and Exchange Commission. (see http://www.financialstabilityboard.org/).

Group of Twenty (G-20): Members of the G-20 consist of the following countries: Argentina, Australia, Brazil, Canada, China, France, Germany, India, Indonesia, Italy, Japan, Mexico, Russia, Saudi Arabia, South Africa, South Korea, Turkey, the United Kingdom, the United States, and the European Union; serves as a forum for advancing international economic cooperation among 20 major advanced and emerging-market countries. Originally established in 1999 to facilitate discussions among the G-20 finance ministers, its prominence increased with the onset of the global financial crisis in the fall of 2008, and the G-20 started meeting at the leader level. In September 2009, G-20 leaders announced that, henceforth, the G-20 would be the "premier" forum for international economic cooperation.

International Monetary Fund (IMF): originated in July 1944, when representatives of 45 countries met in Bretton Woods, New Hampshire, to develop a framework for international economic cooperation. It currently has 188 member countries, and provides policy advice and financing to members in economic difficulties and also works with developing nations to help them achieve macroeconomic stability and reduce poverty. In particular, the IMF: 1) promotes international monetary cooperation and exchange rate stability; 2) provides policy advice to governments and central banks based on analysis of economic trends and cross-country experiences; 3) conducts research, statistics, forecasts, and analysis based on tracking of global, regional, and individual economies and markets; 4) provides loans to help countries overcome economic difficulties; 5) provides concessional loans to help fight poverty in developing countries; and 6) provides technical assistance and training to help countries improve the management of their economies.

International Organization of Securities Commissions (IOSCO): was created in 1983. It sets standards for securities markets. Its membership regulates more than 95% of the world's securities markets and it is the primary international cooperative forum for securities market regulatory agencies.

Legal Entity Identifier (LEI): a program designed to create and apply a single, universal standard identifier to uniquely identify any party to a financial transaction internationally. It helps regulators conduct more accurate analysis of global, systemically important financial institutions and their transactions with all counterparties across markets, products, and regions, allowing regulators to better identify concentrations and emerging risks.

Trade Repositories (TRs): are entities that maintain a centralized electronic record of transaction data. Timely and reliable access to data stored in trade repositories potentially can enhance the transparency of transaction information to relevant authorities and the public to identify and evaluate the potential risks posed to the broader financial system, promote financial stability, and support the detection and prevention of market abuse.

Appendix B. Individual Country Progress in Implementing Derivatives Market Reforms[97]

This Appendix presents detailed information on the progress the G-20 members, except France, Germany, and Italy, which are represented by the European Union, and such FSB members as Singapore and Switzerland, have made in meeting the G-20 self-imposed deadline of adopting reform measures by year-end 2012. The detailed information reflects self-assessments by the individual countries and is cumulative over the four surveys that have been conducted to date. The latest survey was published in October 2012.

Argentina

Standardization. The share of OTC derivatives composed of standardized derivatives is expected to have increased substantially by the end of 2012. Derivatives are traded through Mercado Abierto Electronico (MAE) and two other exchanges, which account for 75% of all derivatives contracts traded in Argentina. Central bank regulations were changed in order to provide for a regulatory stimulus for using guarantees and central clearing parties (CCPs) by all financial institutions supervised by the Central Bank. Argentina argues that it has no need for developing new regulations, but will expand the variety of contracts offered.

Central Clearing. No central clearing. Central bank regulations provide incentives to trade derivatives on organized platforms that provide for central clearing.

Exchange or Electronic Platform Trading. Argentina has a central bank regulation in place that provides incentives to trade derivatives on organized platforms that provide for central clearing. The Comision Nacional de Valores (CNV) regulates the securities markets in Argentina and requires all or any subset of standardized derivatives to be traded on exchanges or electronic trading platforms. MAE, the electronic securities and OTC derivatives trading market in Argentina, is considering increasing the standardized derivative products that can be traded on this platform. CNV requires firm use a common soft for trading negotiable securities that ensures standardization.

Transparency and Trading. Argentina permits a single dealer functionality. Pre-trade price and volume transparency is required for all exchange or electronic-platform-traded and OTC derivatives. Post-trade price and volume transparency is required for all exchanges or electronic-platform-traded and OTC derivatives.

Reporting to Trade Repositories. No laws are in place or are expected to be in place by year-end 2012 that require all OTC derivatives transactions to be reported to trade repositories. Derivatives operations of banks with cross-border counterparties, the bulk of OTC transactions, are subject to reporting and monitoring by the Central Bank. Legislative and/or regulatory steps have been completed toward implementing a reporting requirement. No additional legislative or

---

[97] The details for individual countries in this Appendix are derived from: *OTC Derivatives Market Reforms: Fourth Progress Report on Implementation*, Financial Stability Board, October 31, 2012.

regulatory steps are needed for a reporting requirement to be effective. Regulations require reporting to a governmental authority in place of a specifically-designated trade repository.

Application of Central Clearing Requirements. Derivatives under the jurisdiction of the CNV must be centrally cleared. Central clearing requirements cover all types of financial entities under the jurisdiction of the CNV. Current laws or regulations do not provide for intra-group transactions that are not traded through regulated markets.

Australia

Standardization. The main derivatives traded in Australian markets are interest rate and foreign exchange products, which already are fairly standardized. The Australian government introduced into the Parliament a legislative framework to allow requirements to centrally clear standardized derivatives through central counterparties. Implementing regulations and rules would be necessary before mandatory obligations are imposed. Australian regulators are considering changes to implement Basel III by January 2013.

Central Clearing. Government has introduced legislation to establish a flexible framework for regulators to impose mandatory trade reporting, central clearing, and trade execution obligations on participants, and also establish licensing requirements for trade repositories.

Exchange or Electronic Platform Trading. The government introduced into Parliament a legislative framework to require trading of standardized derivatives on trading platforms or exchanges, with final adoption of the legislation expected by the end of 2012. Implementing regulations and rules need to be developed prior to full implementation of the legislation.

Transparency and Trading. Under current law, which is under review, a single-dealer platform is not required to be regulated as a market. Consequently, under the current market licensing regime if mandatory trading is imposed it would initially be on platforms or markets which offer multi-dealer functionality. Pre-trade price and volume transparency is under review for all exchange or electronic-platform-traded and OTC derivatives. Post-trade price and volume transparency is under review for all exchanges or electronic-platform-traded and OTC derivatives.

Reporting to Trade Repositories. The Australian government introduced into Parliament a legislative framework to allow the imposition of mandatory trade reporting of OTC derivatives. The government expects the legislation to be in effect before the end of 2012, but implementing regulations and rules would be required before any mandatory obligations could be imposed. It also determined that if trade repositories are not available, the legislation would permit the imposition of a requirement that data be reported to a prescribed governmental authority.

Application of Central Clearing Requirements. Australia is developing a framework that does not specify any asset classes that are exempt from the central clearing requirements. However, implementation of any central clearing requirements will be considered on an asset class basis and will likely be harmonized with requirements in major jurisdictions. The framework being adopted does not specify any entities that are exempt from the central clearing requirements. However, implementation of any central clearing requirements likely will be considered on an asset class basis and take into account the impact on financial and non-financial entities.

Coverage will be coordinated with other FSB members. Current laws or regulations for intra-group transactions are under review.

Brazil

Standardization. Brazil's derivatives markets are already highly standardized.

Central Clearing. Existing legislation requires all exchange-traded derivatives to be centrally cleared; non-exchange traded derivatives may be bilaterally risk managed or centrally cleared at the option of the counterparties. Mandatory clearing requirements apply only to exchange-traded derivatives.

Exchange or Electronic Platform Trading. Does not have a law or regulation in place requiring all or any subset of standardized derivatives to be traded on exchanges or electronic trading platforms, but provides capital incentives for use of exchange-traded derivatives.

Transparency and Trading. Multi-dealer functionality is required. Pre-trade price and volume transparency is required for the 90% of the market that is exchange-traded; no pre-trade requirement exists for the 10% of the market that is OTC derivatives. Post-trade price and volume transparency is required for all exchanges or electronic-platform-traded and OTC derivatives.

Reporting to Trade Repositories. Laws currently are in place or are expected to be in place by year-end 2012 that require all OTC derivatives transactions to be reported to trade repositories. Pre-existing laws enacted by the Central Bank and Comissao de Valores Mobiliarios (CVM) (Securities and Exchange Commission of Brazil) require all OTC derivatives trades to be reported to a trade reporter. Also, derivatives transactions must be registered to have legal validity. No additional legislative or regulatory steps are needed for a reporting requirement to be effective. Regulations do not require reporting to a governmental authority in place of a specifically-designated trade repository.

Application of Central Clearing Requirements. Central clearing requirements apply only to exchange-traded derivatives. Current laws or regulations do not provide for intra-group transactions.

Canada

Standardization. The share of OTC derivatives composed of standardized derivatives is expected to have increased substantially by the end of 2012. Canada is considering new capital standards and regulatory steps relative to trading repositories to be implemented indirectly through Basel III capital standards and trade reporting.

Central Clearing. Central clearing is being reviewed with legislation expected before the end of 2012. Legislation is in place in provinces where the majority of OTC derivatives trades are booked, but further work is required to harmonize rules across the provinces. The Canadian Securities Administration is working to identify and implement legislative changes that are needed to support central clearing. Canada is considering a system that would provide for central clearing of systemically important products through a CCP located in Canada for Canadian market participants, with other products cleared offshore. Alternatively, all products could be cleared at existing and planned global CCPs located in Europe or the United States. If this method is adopted, however, Canada supports adopting four safeguards to protect the safety and robustness of the Canadian market: 1) acceptable multilateral cooperative oversight arrangements; 2) satisfactory multi-currency emergency liquidity arrangements; 3) a robust recovery and resolution regime for CCPs; and 4) fair and open access to CCPs.[98]

Exchange or Electronic Platform Trading. Reviewing laws or regulations to require all or any subset of standardized derivatives to be traded on exchanges or electronic trading platforms, and is expected to publish a consultation paper in late 2012 to help develop regulations regarding the impact of a trading requirement.

Transparency and Trading. Canada is developing a process for developing and implementing reporting regulations, with requirements scheduled to be implemented in 2013. The Canadian Securities Administration published a consultation paper on trade repositories and most jurisdictions are assessing what legislative changes may be required. In some provinces, legislation has been proposed. Canada anticipates that a very small number of trades may not be accepted by trade repositories

Reporting to Trade Repositories. Laws will be in place by year-end 2012, depending on legislative changes in rules, to require all OTC derivatives transactions to be reported to trade repositories. The Canadian Securities Administrators published a consultation paper on trade repositories. Most jurisdictions are assessing what legislative changes may be required. Ontario and Quebec have amended legislation to support reporting to trade repositories and regulatory access to the data. It is anticipated that a small number of trades may not be accepted by trade repositories and could be reported to securities regulators.

Application of Central Clearing Requirements. Central clearing requirements for coverage of all the asset classes are under review. Foreign exchange swaps and forwards may be exempted with a view toward harmonizing rules with other jurisdictions. Reviewing coverage of central clearing requirements, particular consideration is being given to systemic risk concerns and harmonization with other jurisdictions. Regarding regulations for intra-group transactions, Canadian securities regulators are considering comments received in response to a consultation paper on en-user exemptions.

China

Standardization. The share of OTC derivatives composed of standardized derivatives is expected to have increased substantially by the end of 2012. China has taken steps to increase the use of standardized products and procedures by adopting an improved Master agreement and Definition document for an electronic trading platform. China has approved the China Foreign Exchange Trading System (CFETS) to introduce standardized post-trade procedures for interest rate swaps.

---

[98] Slive, Joshua, Carolyn Wilkins, and Jonathan Witmer, Access to Central Clearing Services for Over-the-Counter Derivatives, p. 39-45.

Central Clearing. Central clearing is under consideration. Legislation has not been proposed, but the Shanghai Clearing House is being encouraged to establish detailed schemes for central clearing of OTC derivatives and interest rate swaps.

Exchange or Electronic Platform Trading. China is reviewing laws and/or regulations to require all or any subset of standardized derivatives to be traded on exchanges or electronic trading platforms. Has developed an electronic trading platform operated by the China Foreign Exchange Trading System (CFETS). Under regulations developed by the People's Bank of China (PBC), all standardized OTC interest rate and credit derivatives can be traded on the CFETS platform; certain types of derivatives are required to be traded on the CFETS platform.

Transparency and Trading. Multi-dealer functionality is required. Pre-trade price and volume transparency is required for all exchange or electronic-platform-traded and OTC derivatives. Post-trade price and volume transparency is required for all exchanges or electronic-platform-traded and OTC derivatives.

Reporting to Trade Repositories. Laws currently are in place or are expected to be in place by year-end 2012 to require all OTC derivatives transactions to be reported to trade repositories. Under current rules, all OTC interest rate, FX and credit risk mitigation tools (other than credit risk mitigation agreements) can be traded on the China Foreign Exchange Trade System (CFETS) electronic platform; interest rate trades executed outside the CFETS platform are be reported to CFETS. Additional legislative or regulatory steps are needed to determine the frequency and content of reporting and which institution will play the role of trade repositories, Regulations require reporting to a governmental authority in place of a specifically-designated trade repository.

Application of Central Clearing Requirements. Central clearing requirements covering all asset classes are under review. Central clearing requirements for all types of financial entities and requirements for intra-group transactions are yet to be determined.

European Union

Standardization. The share of OTC derivatives composed of standardized derivatives is expected to have increased substantially by the end of 2012. The European Union adopted new regulations through the European Markets Infrastructure Regulation (EMIR). The regulation introduces a reporting obligation for OTC derivatives, a clearing obligation for eligible OTC derivatives, measures to reduce counterparty credit risk and operational risk for bilaterally-cleared OTC derivatives, common rules for central counterparties and for trade repositories, and rules on the establishment of cooperation between central counterparties. The EU also adopted changes to the Capital Requirements Directive to implement the Basel III commitments. The EU is also planning additional amendments to the Markets in Financial Instruments Directive (MiFID) that will include a revised directive covering market structure, exemptions from financial regulation, organizational and conduct of business requirements for investment firms and trade venues, powers of national authorities, sanctions, and rules for third-country firms operating through a branch. The changes to MiFID also include a new regulation which provides requirements for trade transparency, the mandatory trading of derivatives on organized venues and the provision of services by third-country firms without a branch. In addition, the EU has proposed changes to the Markets Abuse Directive (MAD) governing insider trading and information.

Central Clearing. The European Markets Infrastructure Regulation (EMIR) proposal was made in September 2010, which, according to the EU's survey for the FSB, would require all standardized OTC derivatives to be cleared through central counterparties (CCPs). The measure was agreed on in March 2012, with adoption by the European Commission expected by the end of 2012. Additional technical rules are being drafted by the European Securities and Markets Authority (ESMA), the European Banking Authority (EBA), and the European Insurance and Occupational Pensions Authority (EIOPA). The technical standards are expected to be adopted by the end of 2012.

Exchange or Electronic Platform Trading. Currently does not have a law or regulation in place requiring all or any subset of standardized derivatives to be traded on exchanges or electronic trading platforms, but the final rules proposed on MiFID and Markets in Financial Instruments Regulation (MiFIR) are expected to be in effect by mid-2014. Proposed amendments to MiFID would require that the trading of all OTC derivatives, subject to central clearing and which are sufficiently liquid, take place on one of three regulated venues: 1) regulated markets; 2) multilateral trading facilities; and 3) the future organized trading facilities. The amendments are expected to be adopted and technical standards developed for full implementation by mid-2014.

Transparency and Trading. Multi-dealer functionality is proposed as part of the amended MiFid and MiFIR. Pre-trade price and volume transparency is required for all exchange or electronic-platform-traded and OTC derivatives. Post-trade price and volume transparency is required for all exchanges or electronic-platform-traded and OTC derivatives.

Reporting to Trade Repositories. Through the European Markets Infrastructure Regulation (EMIR), laws currently are in place or are expected to be in place by year-end 2012 to require all OTC derivatives transactions to be reported to trade repositories. Technical standards are being developed by the European Securities Markets Authority (ESMA) and are expected to be adopted by the European Commission by year-end 2012. Reporting to the ESMA will be required in instances where a trade repository is not able to record the details of an OTC derivative.

Application of Central Clearing Requirements. Central clearing requirements cover all asset classes. Central clearing requirements cover all types of financial entities, except for a temporary exemption for certain pension arrangements. Current laws or regulations exempt intra-group transactions.

Hong Kong

Standardization. Hong Kong is monitoring developments in the OTC derivatives markets and is consulting with the industry to follow changes. Interest rate swaps and forward contracts (non-deliverable forwards) are already fairly standardized. The Hong Kong Monetary Authority has completed the legislative process for incorporating the Basel III framework into its capital regime for banks for implementation in 2013, which is expected to increase standardization.

Central Clearing. Hong Kong has adopted an interim legislative proposal to support voluntary clearing of certain derivatives transactions through local central clearing parties recognized by the Securities and Futures Commission. Hong Kong is drafting legislative amendments on central clearing with the intent of having them adopted by the end of 2012. Regulators are in the process of fine-tuning a regulatory regime for OTC derivatives, including mandatory clearing requirements.

Exchange or Electronic Platform Trading. A regulatory proposal reviewed by the Legislative Council is being drafted, that will give regulators the authority to impose trading requirements, but the timing of implementing the proposals is subject to further study by regulators. Regulators produced a consultative paper on the proposed OTC derivatives regulatory regime, including a proposal to give regulators authority to make rules to implement a mandatory trading requirement. Hong Kong indicates that it must adopt legislative amendments and engage in further market consultation before finalizing the detailed regulations regarding a mandatory trading requirement.

Transparency and Trading. Dealer functionality is under consideration, with a view toward international developments. Pre-trade price and volume transparency is under consideration for all exchange or electronic-platform-traded and OTC derivatives. Post-trade price and volume transparency is under consideration for all exchanges or electronic-platform-traded and OTC derivatives.

Reporting to Trade Repositories. Laws currently are in place or are expected to be in place by year-end 2012 to require all OTC derivatives transactions to be reported to trade repositories. A regulatory proposal has been reviewed by a committee of the Legislative Council and legislation is being drafted to be adopted in early 2013 to build the regulatory regime for OTC derivatives (pending detailed rules subject to international developments). Hong Kong intends to take a phased approach, beginning with interest rate swaps and non-deliverable forwards. Regulations that require reporting to a governmental authority in place of a specifically-designated trade repository are being developed by the Hong Kong Monetary Authority for submission to the Legislative Council. Legislative amendments must be adopted and further market consultation is also needed before finalizing the detailed regulations on the mandatory reporting requirement. OTC derivatives transactions that have a bearing on Hong Kong's financial market will be required to be reported to the local trade repository to be developed by the Hong Kong Monetary Authority.

Application of Central Clearing Requirements. Central clearing requirements covering all asset classes are being phased in. Mandatory clearing is expected to cover standardized interest rate swaps and non-deliverable forwards initially. Additional measures to extend these clearing requirements eventually to cover other types of instruments will be determined after the initial roll-out. Hong Kong's current proposal is to cover financial institutions holding positions above a certain clearing threshold, which is to be determined. Hong Kong's regulators are prepared to consider the possibility of introducing clearing exemptions in respect of intra-group transactions. Specific details on exemptions from clearing will be provided when the regulators consult on the detailed requirements in early 2013.

India

Standardization. The share of OTC derivatives composed of standardized derivatives is expected to have increased substantially by the end of 2012. The Clearing Corporation of India (CCIL) is expected to start guaranteed settlement in various derivatives. India is planning a gradual approach to developing new legislation. India has achieved standardization relevant to terms of coupon payment, maturity dates, and master agreements for certificates of deposit. Foreign exchange derivatives are essentially standardized.

Central Clearing. No central clearing. India has no had non-guaranteed settlement of interest rate swaps since November 2008. Despite not having requirements that interest rate swaps be centrally cleared, 70% of such derivatives are centrally cleared. India is taking progressive steps toward the central clearing of OTC derivatives transactions. India is transitioning to a system of guaranteed settlement of interest rate swaps, but has no immediate timeframe for the guaranteed settlement of credit default swaps.

Exchange or Electronic Platform Trading. India does not have a law or regulation in place requiring all or any subset of standardized derivatives to be traded on exchanges or electronic trading platforms. India, however, has mandated a trading requirement for all repurchase agreements in government securities, interest rate swaps, forward rate agreements, and foreign exchange forwards. Explicit authority is required to approve OTC derivatives trading platforms.

Transparency and Trading. Post-trade price and volume transparency is required for all exchanges or electronic-platform-traded and OTC derivatives. Single dealer and multi-dealer facilities are available for foreign exchange derivatives.

Reporting to Trade Repositories. Laws currently are in place or are expected to be in place by year-end 2012 to require all OTC derivatives transactions to be reported to trade repositories. Banks and primary dealers should report interest rate swaps (IRS) and forward rate agreements (FRA) and foreign exchange derivatives transactions to the CCIL reporting platform. Credit default swaps (CDS) all market makers must report trades on the centralized reporting platform within the stipulated time after execution of the trade. In addition to regulatory guidelines adopted in 2007 and 2011, India issued regulatory guidelines in 2012 for reporting trades of certain forwards, swaps, and options. India is considering a phased in approach to bring any remaining OTC derivatives under the reporting framework. Recommendations have been made to the Financial Sector Legislative Reform Commission to provide appropriate statutory authority for the regulation of trade repositories and for facilitating reporting to and dissemination of information from trade repositories to the appropriate members and regulators. India does not require reporting to a government authority in place of a specifically-designated trade repository. Interest rate swaps are being reported to the CCIL and the details are accessible to the Reserve Bank of India.

Application of Central Clearing Requirements. Central clearing facility is available for interest rate swaps, foreign exchange forwards, and repurchase agreements in government securities. Central clearing for credit default swaps is being considered, depending on market developments. Central clearing requirements cover all types of financial entities. Current laws or regulations provide for intra-group transactions, provided that the accounts are held separately.

Indonesia

Standardization. The share of OTC derivatives composed of standardized derivatives is expected to have increased substantially by the end of 2012. Indonesia has approved the exchange trading of standardized derivatives products on the Surabaya Stock Exchange since 2003. Rules on futures contracts and options on securities or on indexes must be traded on an exchange. Indonesia is expected to consider additional legislation in the 2013-2015 timeframe.

Central Clearing. Currently, derivatives trading in Indonesia is a relatively low volume activity and takes place only on exchanges, There are no plans to establish a central clearing requirements for OTC derivatives.

Exchange or Electronic Platform Trading. Indonesia does not have a law or regulation that requires all or any subset of standardized derivatives to be traded on exchanges or electronic trading platforms. Also, Indonesia does have a rule in place on futures contracts and options on securities or on securities indexes. A revision of the current rules is expected in 2012-2013.

Transparency and Trading. Multi-dealer functionality is required. Pre-trade price and volume transparency is required for all exchange or electronic-platform-traded and OTC derivatives. Post-trade price and volume transparency is required for all exchanges or electronic-platform-traded and OTC derivatives.

Reporting to Trade Repositories. In Indonesia, derivatives can only be traded on exchanges. Current regulations require that OTC derivative transactions be reported to trade repositories. That requirement, however, covers only debt instruments (non-derivatives). Banks are required to report interest rate derivatives and foreign exchange derivatives to the central bank. There are no proposed changes to laws or regulations.

Application of Central Clearing Requirements. Central clearing requirements are under review. Central clearing requirements for all types of financial entities are under review.

Japan

Standardization. A considerable portion of Japan's derivatives markets is already standardized. Japan amended its Financial Instruments and Exchange Act in May 2010 to improve stability and transparency in the settlement of OTC derivatives and in September 2012 for the use of an electronic trading platform. A Cabinet Office Ordinance was adopted and is being implemented on central counterparties; use of an electronic trading platform is expected to be phased in over three years.

Central Clearing. Initially, central clearing requirements will apply only to yen interest rate swaps and credit default swaps. Japan's Financial Instruments and Exchange Act (FIEA) was amended in May 2010, as a step toward mandating clearing of standardized derivatives. Also, a Cabinet Ordinance will be implemented by November 2012 that will include a requirement for a central clearing parties to clear trades "that are significant in volume and would reduce settlement risks in the domestic market."

Exchange or Electronic Platform Trading. Legislation was adopted that amended the Financial Instruments and Exchange Act requiring the use of exchange or electronic trading platforms. The changes are expected to be phased in over a period up to three years.

Transparency and Trading. Multi-dealer functionality is expected, but single-dealer functionality is accepted. Pre-trade price and volume transparency is being determined for all exchange or electronic-platform-traded and OTC derivatives. Post-trade price and volume transparency is being determined for all exchanges or electronic-platform-traded and OTC derivatives.

Reporting to Trade Repositories. Laws currently are in place or are expected to be in place by year-end 2012 to require all OTC derivatives transactions to be reported to trade repositories. The Financial Instruments and Exchange Act was amended to introduce the legislative framework for reporting OTC derivatives transactions to trade repositories. Trade data not reported to trade repositories, primarily data on exotic OTC derivatives, will be reported to the Japan Financial Services Authority (JFSA). A Cabinet ordinance is expected to be completed by November 2012. Data reported to JFSA will be limited to information not accepted by a trade repository, such as exotic OTC derivatives trades.

Application of Central Clearing Requirements. A Cabinet Ordinance on central clearing requirements for all asset classes is expected to be implemented by November 2012. Initially, the requirements will apply to Yen interest rate swaps and certain credit default swaps. After November 2012, applicable products will be further expanded based on a review. Central clearing requirements apply to major "Financial Intermediaries Business Operations" and financial institutions. The new Cabinet Ordinance is not expected to cover intra-group transactions.

Mexico

Standardization. Most OTC derivatives products are already highly standardized. Mexican financial authorities are developing a general framework on financial markets that is expected to be concluded by year-end 2012. Financial authorities are considering specific legislation to regulate derivatives markets.

Central Clearing. Mexican authorities expect to enact a law and or secondary regulations to require all standardized OTC derivatives be cleared through central counterparties. The Mexican Financial Authority is expected to develop a general framework and submit it for approval by the legislature.

Exchange or Electronic Platform Trading. Authorities plan to enact a law and secondary regulation relative to a subset of standardized derivatives that are to be traded on electronic trading platforms. Financial authorities also are developing a general framework based on the amendments to the secondary regulation to be concluded in 2012. In addition to the regulatory framework, the financial authorities are considering the need for specific legislation to regulate derivatives markets.

Transparency and Trading. Multi-dealer functionality is required. Pre-trade price and volume transparency is not required for all exchange or electronic-platform-traded and OTC derivatives. Post-trade price and volume transparency is required for all exchanges or electronic-platform-traded and OTC derivatives.

Reporting to Trade Repositories. Authorities plan to enact laws or secondary regulations to require all OTC derivatives transactions be reported to a trade repository. Under current law, banks report OTC derivatives transactions to the Central Bank; legislation is expected to be adopted that will require all OTC derivatives transactions to be reported to trade repositories by year-end 2012. Financial authorities are developing a general framework based on amendments to the secondary regulations to be completed by year-end 2012. In addition, financial authorities are considering developing specific new legislation to regulate the derivatives market. Currently, local financial intermediaries are required to report OTC derivatives to local authorities, but financial authorities intend to have entities report to specifically-designated trade repositories.

Application of Central Clearing Requirements. As an initial step, peso-denominated interest rate swaps (currently 90% of the domestic OTC derivatives) will be subject to mandatory central clearing. All derivatives determined as standardized by the Central Bank will be subject to the central clearing requirement. Initially, central clearing requirements will only apply to banks and brokerage houses. Current laws or regulations do not provide for intra-group transactions and no exemptions are planned.

South Korea

Standardization. The share of OTC derivatives composed of standardized derivatives is expected to have increased substantially by the end of 2012. Amended its Financial Investment Services and Capital Markets Act to include standardization of OTC derivatives. Additional amendments are expected to be submitted to the National Assembly related to enforcement of ordinances and supervisory regulations.

Central Clearing. Central clearing is in place, but the National Assembly is expected to adopt amendments to the Financial Investment Services and Capital Markets Act to provide detailed provisions of enforcement ordinances and supervisory regulations and the establishment and pilot-testing of domestic central clearing.

Exchange or Electronic Platform Trading. South Korea does not have a law or regulation in place requiring all or any subset of standardized derivatives to be traded on exchanges or electronic trading platforms. Currently, it is reviewing its policy options.

Transparency and Trading. Multi-dealer functionality is required. Pre-trade price and volume transparency is required for all exchange or electronic-platform-traded and OTC derivatives. Post-trade price and volume transparency is required for all exchanges or electronic-platform-traded and OTC derivatives.

Reporting to Trade Repositories. Laws currently are in place or are expected to be in place by year-end 2012 to require all OTC derivatives transactions to be reported to trade repositories. The Financial Investment Services and Capital Markets Act and the Foreign Exchange Transactions Act require the reporting of all OTC derivatives transactions to authorities. Additional legislative or regulatory steps are needed to improve some parts of the reporting system to meet international standards. Current regulations require reporting to a governmental authority in place of a specifically-designated trade repository.

Application of Central Clearing Requirements. Central clearing requirements cover all asset classes. Central clearing requirements cover all types of financial entities.

Russia

Standardization. Russia adopted laws on clearing and clearing services that creates a legal basis for a Master agreement, standardized OTC contracts and tax preferences for agreements on standardized terms. Certain tax preferences apply only to agreements on standard terms and close-out netting. As a first step, it introduced classification codes for OTC derivatives. Implementing regulations expected to be in place by year-end 2012.

Central Clearing. Existing laws provide for clearing and clearing services and create a legal basis for adopting regulations dealing with central clearing of standardized OTC derivatives. Russia is implementing regulations that are needed to implement central clearing, including close-put netting of contracts concluded under a Master Agreement and aligning close-out netting rules with the Master Agreement.

Exchange or Electronic Platform Trading. Russia has adopted a law requiring platform trading of all or any subset of standardized derivatives. It is gaining practical experiences before proceeding with further regulatory measures. Current laws provide authority to adopt implementing regulations.

Transparency and Trading. Dealer functionality is being determined. Pre-trade price and volume transparency is required only for exchange-traded derivatives. Post-trade price and volume transparency is being determined for all exchanges or electronic-platform-traded and OTC derivatives.

Reporting to Trade Repositories. Laws currently are in place or are expected to be in place by year-end 2012 that will require those transactions that are conducted by professional market participants and transactions that are subject to close-out netting and that are executed under Master Agreements be reported to trade repositories. Such transactions as corporate repurchase agreements, derivatives, and other securities must provide a repository with the information on the transactions. The repository is responsible for maintaining a register of the transactions and for providing the register to the Federal Financial Markets Service. Additional legislative or regulatory steps are needed for a reporting requirement to be effective. Regulations require reporting to a governmental authority in place of a specifically-designated trade repository.

Application of Central Clearing Requirements. Central clearing requirements cover all asset classes. Central clearing requirements cover all types of financial entities. Current laws or regulations cover intra-group transactions.

Saudi Arabia

Standardization. Banks already use standardized contracts, known as Customer Treasury Agreements (CTA). A revised version of the CTA is being developed that will incorporate the International Swaps and Derivatives Association (ISDA) and International Islamic Financial Markets standards and Tahawwut (Hedging) Master Agreement (TMA) to standardize sharia law compliant swap-based hedging transactions. The adoption and implementation of the TMA agreement and the requirement by the Saudi Arabian Monetary Authority (SAMA) for all counterparties to use the TMA in place of the CTA will ensure that all counterparties will use a standard contract.

Central Clearing. Regulations for central clearing have not been proposed, but the issue is being examined by the Saudi banking authority. A self-assessment conducted by Saudi Arabia indicated that the current and future trading volumes of derivatives are unlikely to justify establishing a domestic clearing counterparty (CCP). Instead, the Saudi Bank is being encouraged to establish clearing relationships with global CCPs.

Exchange or Electronic Platform Trading. Saudi Arabia does not have laws or regulations that require all or any subset of standardized derivatives to be traded on exchanges or electronic trading platforms. Saudi Arabia has determined to establish a local Trade Repository under the supervision of the Saudi Arabian Monetary Authority. The proposed TR will provide a mechanism for increasing transparency of OTC derivatives market activity, commitments, and balances. the TR is also expected to serve as the future foundation for any electronic trading on exchanges should the need for such a mechanism arise. Saudi Arabia contends that the TR in tandem with the standardization of the OTC market through the TMA will address regulatory requirements for greater transparency and disclosure.

Transparency and Trading. Saudi Arabia has determined that the existing and future volumes do not require setting up electronic trading of exchanges. A self-assessment indicates that the volumes currently be traded do not require pre-trade price and volume transparency or post-trade price and volume transparency for all exchanges or electronic-platform-traded and OTC derivatives.

Reporting to Trade Repositories. As a result of a self-assessment, Saudi Arabia is planning on establishing a trade repository under the supervision of the Saudi Arabian Monetary Authority. Officials expect that appropriate regulations will be in place by year-end 2012 to require all OTC derivatives transactions to be reported to trade repositories.

Application of Central Clearing Requirements. Central clearing requirements are under review. Central clearing requirements covering all types of financial entities are under review; intra-group transactions are under review.

Singapore

Standardization. Major dealers in the market are the 14 dealers committed to the "roadmap" plan to increase standardization. Singapore has considered draft legislation to implement Basel III capital requirements and has finalized provisions to be implemented by the end of 2012.

Central Clearing. Central clearing is in place. Public consultation concerning proposed policies governing central clearing is expected to be followed by legislation by year-end 2012.

Exchange or Electronic Platform Trading. Singapore is expected to introduce legislation in 2012 that will require all or any subset of standardized derivatives to be traded on exchanges or electronic trading platforms.

Transparency and Trading. Pre-trade price and volume transparency is not yet determined for all exchange or electronic-platform-traded and OTC derivatives. Post-trade price and volume transparency is being determined for all exchanges or electronic-platform-traded and OTC derivatives.

Reporting to Trade Repositories. Laws currently are in place or are expected to be in place by year-end 2012 to require all OTC derivatives transactions to be reported to trade repositories. Legislation is expected to be introduced by year-end 2012 to implement reporting and licensing requirements. Officials are developing detailed regulations, subject to international developments.

Application of Central Clearing Requirements. Central clearing requirements cover all asset classes, accounting for systemic risk to the local market and the degree of standardization in the local market. Central clearing requirements will cover all types of financial entities and non-financial entities above a specified threshold that are licensed and regulated by the Monetary Authority of Singapore. Measures being considered would exempt intra-group transactions, subject to the application of stringent risk mitigation requirements.

South Africa

Standardization. South Africa has adopted a phased-in approach, although the increased use of standardized OTC derivatives is intended, but not expected to increase substantially by the end of 2012. The South Africa Financial Services Board amended its Securities Services Act to strengthen the regulation of unlisted securities, which includes OTC derivatives. A Financial Markets Bill was adopted to improve market supervision, provide additional protections to investors, and to regulate financial markets to be fair, efficient, and transparent.

Central Clearing. Central clearing is in place. A Financial Markets Bill establishing central clearing procedures was submitted to the National Treasury for Cabinet and Parliamentary approval. The Financial Markets Bill and implementing regulations are expected to be adopted by the end of 2012.

Exchange or Electronic Platform Trading. South Africa does not have a law or regulation in place requiring all or any subset of standardized derivatives to be traded on exchanges or electronic trading platforms. Currently does not anticipate that electronic trading of OTC derivatives will be required.

Transparency and Trading. No decision has been made regarding requirements for electronic trading of OTC derivatives. If a decision is made to require electronic trading, regulators will consider the characteristics of eligible platforms, developments in other jurisdictions, and guidance from the International Organization of Securities Commissions (IOSCO). Post-trade price and volume transparency is required for all exchanges or electronic-platform-traded derivatives, but not for OTC derivatives until they are traded on an exchange.

Reporting to Trade Repositories. The Financial Markets Bill (FMB) was submitted for approval by the Treasury, Cabinet and the Parliament that will establish reporting requirements. The FMB and additional legislation is expected to be in effect by the end of 2012.

Application of Central Clearing Requirements. Central clearing requirements are under review. Central clearing coverage requirements are under review. Current laws or regulations regarding intra-group transactions are under review.

Switzerland

Standardization. Switzerland has experienced a greater use of standardized derivatives, it two major banks have committed to increase their use of standardized contracts, and it is making adjustments to comply with the Basel III capital requirements. The Swiss Federal Council decided on a legislative reform package to fully implement the FSB principles regarding OTC derivatives and to improve the regulation of financial market infrastructures. The draft legislation is scheduled for public consultation through the end of 2012.

Central Clearing. Central clearing is not yet in place, but legislation is in progress. Draft legislation has been approved by the Swiss Federal Council and is expected to be implemented by the end of 2012 that will implement the FSB principles in the area of OTC derivatives and amend the regulation of financial market infrastructure.

Exchange or Electronic Platform Trading. Switzerland's Stock Exchange Act requires exchanges to establish a trade repository of trade details and to publish quotes and volumes of on-exchange and off-exchange transactions; for collateralized certificates. Switzerland has introduced collateralized securities instruments (COSI) services to allow for automated trading, clearing without risk transfer, and settlement of these instruments. Application to OTC derivatives trading is currently under review. The Swiss Federal Council has decided on a legislative reform package to fully implement the FSB principles in the area of OTC derivatives and to improve the regulation of financial market infrastructure based on the analysis of a working group. Draft legislation is scheduled for public consultation in the first half of 2013.

Transparency and Trading. Pre-trade price and volume transparency is under review for all exchanges or electronic-platform-traded and OTC derivatives. Post-trade price and volume transparency is under review for all exchanges or electronic-platform-traded and OTC derivatives. Exchanges currently are required to provide pre-trade transparency.

Reporting to Trade Repositories. The legislative process is progressing toward adopting measures to require all OTC derivatives transactions to be reported to trade repositories. The Stock Exchanges and Securities Trading Act (SESTA) applies to derivatives traded on exchanges and requires securities dealers to report all the necessary information to ensure a transparent market. The Swiss Federal Council decided on a legislative reform package to fully implement the FSB principles in the area of OTC derivatives and to improve the regulation of financial market infrastructures. Draft legislation is scheduled for public consultation in the first half of 2013. Regulations are under review to require reporting to a governmental authority in place of a specifically-designated trade repository.

Application of Central Clearing Requirements. Swiss authorities are reviewing central clearing requirements with consideration toward covering. Central clearing requirements that cover all types of financial entities are under review. Current laws or regulations for intra-group transactions are under review.

Turkey

Standardization. Investment firms are prohibited from trading in OTC derivatives, while banks use standardized derivatives with standardized features. A draft Capital Markets Law was submitted to the Parliament to introduce OTC derivatives as capital market instruments. It is expected to be adopted by early 2013. Additional measures are being reviewed to prepare a legislative framework that complies with the FSB principles.

Central Clearing. No central clearing is in place, but the Capital Markets Law was introduced in Parliament in July 2012 and is expected to be adopted. The measure will allow the Capital Markets Board to designate clearing agents to centrally clear OTC derivatives transactions or to require the establishment of central counterparties in certain markets. A working group has been established to develop a legislative proposal to comply with the FSB principles.

Exchange or Electronic Platform Trading. Policy options are under review.

Transparency and Trading. Pre-trade price and volume transparency is under review for all exchange or electronic-platform-traded and OTC derivatives. Post-trade price and volume transparency is under review for all exchanges or electronic-platform-traded and OTC derivatives.

Reporting to Trade Repositories. A proposed Capital Markets Law that was introduced to the Parliament will give the Capital Markets Board (CMB) the authority to require capital markets transactions, including OTC derivatives, to be reported directly to the CMB or to an authorized trade repository. Although not currently required, equity linked OTC derivatives transactions and leveraged foreign exchange transactions are reported to the Istanbul Stock Exchange (ISE) or the ISE Custody and Settlement Bank. Legislation is under review to implement a reporting requirement. A working group was established to prepare a legislative framework that is consistent with FSB principles. The proposed Capital Markets Law is expected to give the CMB the authority to require capital markets transactions, including OTC derivatives, to be reported directly to the CMB or to an authorized TR.

Application of Central Clearing Requirements. Turkish authorities are reviewing if central clearing requirements cover all asset classes. Authorities are also reviewing central clearing requirements covering all types of financial entities. Current laws or regulations for intra-group transactions are under review.

United States

Standardization. The share of OTC derivatives composed of standardized derivatives is expected to have increased substantially by the end of 2012. The Commodity Futures Trading Commission (CFTC) and the Securities and Exchange Commission (SEC) developed implementing rules as a result of the Dodd–Frank Wall Street Reform and Consumer Protection Act (P.L. 111-203) regarding processes for determining whether specific derivatives contracts will be subject to mandatory clearing. The CFTC finalized a rule that establishes a schedule for compliance with mandatory clearing requirements for swaps and proposed new rules to require that swaps in four interest rate swap classes and two credit default swap classes be required to be cleared by registered derivatives clearing organizations. The CFTC and SEC have proposed, but not finalized, additional rules designed to promote standardization. Final rules by the CFTC and the SEC are expected to be adopted, including CFTC rules to establish processes to determine whether swaps have been made available to trade and consequently subject to mandatory execution on designated contract markets or swap execution facilities.

Central Clearing. With adoption of the Dodd-Frank Act in July 2010, the United States has a law in force requiring all standardized OTC derivatives to be cleared through CCPs, according to the FSB assessment. The CFTC and SEC have adopted final rules regarding processes related to determining whether specific derivatives contracts will be subject to mandatory clearing. The CFTC finalized a rule establishing a schedule for compliance with mandatory clearing requirements and proposed new rules to require that swaps in four interest rate swap classes and two credit default swap classes be required to be cleared by registered derivatives clearing organizations. The CFTC also has finalized rules on clearing documentation, the timing for acceptance of cleared trades, core principles applicable to CFTC-registered derivatives, clearing organizations, and the exception to mandatory clearing for certain non-financial entities using swaps to hedge or mitigate commercial risk.

Exchange or Electronic Platform Trading. The United States has completed a legislative step toward implementing a trading requirement for standardized derivatives, as the Dodd-Frank Act requires any swap or security-based swap subject to the clearing requirement to be traded on a registered trading platform, such as an exchange or swap execution facility registered with the CFTC, or security-based swap execution facility registered with the SEC. The CFTC has finalized rules and regulations with regard to designated contract markets. In addition, the CFTC has proposed regulations with regard to swap execution facilities and regulations defining the process by which a swap is "made available to trade," by a designated contract market or swap execution facility. The SEC has proposed rules pertaining to the registration and operation of trading platforms. Final rules must be implemented for the trading requirement to be effective, the FSB assessment found.

Transparency and Trading. Multi-dealer functionality is required. Pre-trade price and volume transparency is being determined for all exchange or electronic-platform-traded and OTC derivatives. Post-trade price and volume transparency is required for all exchanges or electronic-platform-traded and OTC derivatives. The Dodd-Frank Act required that market participants have the ability to execute or trade swaps or security-based swaps subject to clearing and trading mandates by accepting bids and offers made by multiple participants on an exchange or swap execution facility. The CFTC and SEC have proposed rules to implement this requirement, the FSB assessment found.

Reporting to Trade Repositories. There are laws currently in place that require all OTC derivatives transactions to be reported to trade repositories, according to the FSB assessment. The main legislative approach is through the Dodd-Frank Act, adopted in July 2010. The CFTC has finalized registration requirements, duties, and core principles applicable to CFTC-regulated TRs and rules on the reporting of swaps to TRs, including swaps entered into before the Dodd-Frank Act was enacted and which had not expired and swaps entered into on or after the date of enactment but prior to the relevant reporting compliance date. Compliance with these rules will be phased-in by swap class starting in fall 2012 with credit and interest rate swaps. The CFTC also has designated a provider of legal entity identities to be used by registered entities and swap counterparties in complying with the CFTC's swap data reporting regulations and continues to assist the industry's efforts in the development of a Universal Product Identifier and product classification protocol. The SEC has proposed implementing regulations towards this reporting requirement and specifying registration requirements, duties, and core principles of SEC-regulated TRs. Reporting to a governmental authority in place of a specifically-designated trade repository is expected to be limited in scope, should no trade repository be available, the FSB survey found.

Application of Central Clearing Requirements. Central clearing requirements cover all asset classes, although the Department of the Treasury has proposed exempting foreign exchange swaps and forwards from mandatory clearing requirements. Central clearing requirements cover all types of financial entities, although the CFTC has adopted a final rule that exempts banks, savings associations, farm credit system institutions, and credit unions with total assets of $10 billion or less from the definition of "financial entity," making such "small financial institutions" eligible to elect to use the end-use exception to mandatory clearing for swaps that hedge or mitigate commercial risk. A similar exemption for such entities is being considered by the SEC. The SEC is considering an inter-affiliate clearing exemption, while the CFTC has proposed an inter-affiliate clearing exemption.

Author Contact Information

James K. Jackson
Specialist in International Trade and Finance
jjackson@crs.loc.gov, 7-7751

Rena S. Miller
Analyst in Financial Economics
rsmiller@crs.loc.gov, 7-0826